You Won't Re

SBY
Happy Travels!

Ann[?]

You Won't Remember This

Travel with Babies

Edited by Sandy Bennett-Haber

Published by Flamingo Rover in 2016
Orwell Place, Edinburgh
www.travelswithbaby.co.uk

Typeset by Hewer Text UK Ltd, Edinburgh
Cover design by Jenny Proudfoot

Published in paperback and digital formats

British Library Cataloguing-in-Publication Data
A catalogue record for this book is available from the British Library

ISBN 978-1-910437-12-4

To my boys Rafa and Finn –

And to Blossom and Tilly and all those babies
and families who did not get to journey together.

Contents Page

Introduction

In June 2014 – with the magic combination of maternity leave, my mum over from Australia and my ten month old getting into a good sleeping routine – I dreamed up the idea of this book. And more importantly I believed I could pull it off.

The idea came to me in that quiet time while I was lying with Raphael as he drifted off to sleep for the night. During the past few days (with my mother's help) I had carved out time to work on a travel story about a recent trip to the Isle of Mull. It was for a newspaper competition and I was pleased to have finished it on deadline. I went on the trip with my mum and my son, but wrote them out of the story in order to conform to my idea of a 'travel' story. Surely, I reasoned – solo adventurers are far more appealing to readers and editors than strung out mummies.

As I lay with my Rafa, the centre of my universe, who I had spent the last few days editing out, it popped into my head to wonder if there was an avenue for publishing travel pieces *with* babies. I had seen a Facebook picture of my friend Lydia and her son Eden on an elephant in Thailand, so I knew I wasn't the only parent tucking their child under their arm and heading off on adventures. I wanted to know more about that story and I wondered if others might as well.

Thus on the basis of having travel tales which featured Rafa to tell, and knowing one other person who was likely to have a baby – travel tale of her own, I decided search out a book's worth of tales. In homage to the book's genesis my contribution to the collection is that Isle of Mull tale, with my mum and Rafa edited back in. Lydia was one of the earliest respondents to my first call out for stories – sending a riveting account of her Thai adventures. I read her story on my phone as I pushed the pram home from a supermarket outing. Even her quickly put together notes had me transported away from the leafy Edinburgh street I was walking along – and strengthened my belief in the idea for the travel with babies book.

Fast forward to the end of June 2015, and I am on a lumpy bunk bed in the Peak District breast feeding my nearly two month old son Finlay. Rafa is crying snotty distressed toddler tears in the travel cot wedged under the window, while the early evening sun streams through the thin curtain and people outside chat over their beers. I curse the hare brained idea of travelling with two small babies and wish myself back on the life raft of our home routine: breakfast, playground, home for a nap followed by a frolic in the garden, then inside for the babies' dinner, bath, bed, with the reward of a TV dinner whilst the two babies sleep. That few hours watching telly and folding the laundry hovers before me all day. It is my 'me' recharge time before I crawl into bed to grab some sleep between night feeds.

The evening wears on and sleep continues to elude the boys. Overtired twenty-two month old Rafa thrashes around and hits his head on the bunk bed as I try to settle him. Childless friends troop noisily up and down the stairs outside and the just barely settled baby wakes up again. In the sliver of my brain not overrun by the demands of grizzly unsettled children I question how I could ever have thought publishing a book of stories about travelling with babies could be a good idea. I have been both humbled and inspired by the highly personal journeys contributed to this collection, and the fluttering panic of 'how will I ever find time to get the book finished,' assails me regularly. But a deeper panic exists as well, what if I get it finished, and someone somewhere in the future gets themselves into their own nightmarish pickle because they read a book about travelling with babies and think 'Hey, yeah, we should give that a go.'

In the four hours it takes my husband and I to get the two of them to sleep other travel low-lights haunt me: there was that camping trip just before Rafa stopped breast feeding, where the tent was so cold he would only sleep while one of us sat up holding him; there was that time my husband and Rafa got stuck in the car all night waiting to be towed; and there was that time the blueberries ran out before take off and nearly two year old Rafa cried for forty minutes, while pregnant mummy held him in her 'straightjacket hold' waiting for him to go to sleep. I swear (not for the first time) that I am never ever going anywhere again.

In the slightly more calm light of day some of the benefits of our trip shine through. Yes, we all ended up in tears at bedtime, but there are tears at home too. There was a memorable female solidarity moment in our shabby bunk-room: a friend fed her baby in an adjoining bunk while another pal fed us medicinal red wine. Over breakfast there are adults to chat with, kids and adults to play with Rafa and coo over Finn. Our friend Vicky takes the boys for a walk while I go for a morning run with my husband. I enjoy life away from the small flat, the laundry and the TV. The run and the company and the different horizon help remind me how the quiet settled little life, that I wished myself back into last night, can sometimes be an anchor – dragging on mummy's sanity – and the best relief is throwing the routine out the window.

Some days with babies the world seems very small and it is refreshingly invigorating to be reminded that the world is big, and that you can still embrace it when you have a baby strapped to your front. Many people looked at us askance when we said we were going travelling with our baby – we even tried to buy a plane ticket for Rafa before he was born (apparently you can't do that) – we did not know any different. We believed we could do it. We did it. We loved it.

And yet with the terrible twos on us and a new baby as well, I survive by clinging to our routine. Often my own experience tells me anything else is too hard; on those days the recollection of the brave, mad endeavours of other passionate travellers and parents helps me to get out the front door. On a day when getting the laundry and the babies down the stairs to the garden was a challenging 'outing' I received Erin Mckittrick's glimpse of her life lived large in Alaska, which closes this collection, and my pulse raced as the big wide world beckoned again.

Sandy Bennett-Haber
Edinburgh, January 2016.

Pumpkin Baby

Anne Hamilton

Bangladesh

'**H**ow much is your baby?'

The middle-aged man, dressed in a white shirt, navy suit jacket and a fraying lunghi that appears to be sewn from pink gingham tea towels, wipes his bare feet carefully on the edge of the deck and comes to stand in front of me.

'Excuse me?' I may not have heard him properly. Twilight is the busiest time at the ghat. Hawkers and traders are intent on selling the last of their oranges or cauliflowers or chickens and the already over-crowded, overnight launches are jostling for the limited berths prior to their journeys across the Bay of Bengal. Warm diesel, rotting fruit and dead fish assault the nostrils as much as the shouting, sirens and engines bother the eardrums. My mind is half on shielding the baby at my breast from fascinated fellow-passengers, half on adding this place: Sadharghat, Dhaka, Bangladesh, to the lengthening list of Places My Nipples Have Seen: a travelogue with a difference.

'How much is your baby?' the man says; politely, patiently, and again in Bangla for the crowd that has been drifting around me for the last hour. 'How much is your baby?'

I have heard him correctly and so has the nodding audience. I look around for Ali, friend and guide, bringer of order to chaos and interpreter extraordinaire, but his mission to barter for bread and bananas has taken him to the far side of the river.

'My baby is not for sale.' I try to strike a note between friendly conversation and maternal protectiveness. It must involve an unconscious drawing of said baby further to my bosom, because he, Simon, gives his own indignant squeak and struggles to sit up.

The crowd gives an impressed murmur.

'A fine healthy baby,' the man approves.

'Yes, isn't he?' I say, proud mama momentarily distracted. Simon isn't a delicate newborn, the impression he might give when burrowing beneath my dupatta – never has a salwar kameez and all its flowing accoutrements been so usefully modest – all screwed up in an attempt to guzzle as much milk as he can, as quickly as he can. He's like the hungriest piglet in the litter, except, thank goodness, there is only one of him. At a whopping year old he shows no sign of ever relinquishing breast milk.

'But he's still not for sale.' I'm more firm this time.

'Baby not for sale,' the man repeats. Then he laughs so loudly I can see a gold filling, three blackened teeth and gums crimson from chewing paan. He addresses the swelling crowd and they roar with laughter too. Not to be left out, so does Simon. The hilarity goes on for quite a while, until the man reaches down and dabs his eyes with the edge of his lunghi.

'Apa,' he says. 'I do not wish to buy your baby. . .'

Cue more canned laughter.

'. . .I ask how much he is?' He holds his hands out, palms up and moves them alternately up and down in a hefting motion.

The apposite penny drops.

'Ah. You mean, how much does my baby weigh?'

'Apa, yes, yes,' the man beams, and the crowd gives me a round of applause, 'that is what I say. How much is he weight?'

My maternal credibility takes a nosedive. 'I don't know,' I admit. 'I haven't weighed him for a while.'

I watch the man compute this. He clicks his fingers, apparently catches the eye of someone behind me and fires off an unfathomable round of Bangla. Willing hands pass an orange plastic chair over their heads so that the man can sit down, centre-stage, beside Simon and me. He removes his jacket, places it neatly over the back of his seat and smooths down his lunghi.

'I am Nazrul,' he says. 'Will you take tea?'

I've learned a lot about Bangladesh over the decade or so I've been coming here. I may have a hilarious take on the language, be incapable of preventing my dupatta sweeping the floor, and am frequently challenged by slurping such delicacies as fish larvae or crown of rooster soup, but I do know that when a new friend offers tea, the answer is yes, even if your heart and bowel scream no. Equally, I know that drinking tea on a launch, where the pot is filled from the river and heated to tepid with a generous splash of condensed milk, is an invitation to acute, prolific, stomach-gurgling-for-a-week, horror-story-to-tell-for-the-rest-of-your-life diarrhoea.

Hmm.

Asking for Coca-Cola instead is a sure-fire get out of jail free card, but does require gauging your host's ability to afford it; a man with a posh suit jacket and a faded cotton lunghi on the public deck of a boat pensioned off from India (via Eastern Europe) is too much of an enigma.

'Lovely,' I say, 'thank you.'

He nods and we sit in companionable silence, watched by the crowd. The boatmen, the hawkers and embarking passengers go about their business. Occasionally, I see something like a motorcycle or a generator being hauled on deck, but mostly it's baskets of tomatoes or sacks of rice on the heads of the passers-by who pause to swell the ranks of our crowd. No sign of Ali, but since he got us here about half a day early for the night voyage, I guess he'll vault on deck before we actually heave anchors or whatever ferries do.

After lots of meerkat minutes – the crowd poised for Simon or me to do something and us poised for them to do something – there's a ripple like a Mexican wave and Mr Nazrul jumps up. I expect to see the tea tray appearing at the top of the stairs, but unless it's one prepared for a giant, I'm mistaken. On the drooping shoulders of a convoy of four grinning little boys comes a set of brass-coloured weighing scales, the old-fashioned ones you might once have seen in a chemist-shop window, deco-rated with little weights and measures. The crowd parts and the boys reverently lower the whole contraption and set it upright; it is enormous. I would ask where on earth it came from, but this is Bangladesh; bizarre stuff just happens.

'I tell you how much for your baby,' Mr Nazrul says, rubbing his hands in a way that makes gleeful seem like an understatement.

I must look confused, or incredulous, because:

'For your baby weight,' he explains. 'How much he is. What he weight. . .'

'Okay,' I interrupt, as this could clearly go on for some time, 'You want to weigh Simon.' 'Yes, apa, yes,' he smiles. Then his face creases, 'there is a problem?' he asks.

I'm in a country where I have been on a hijacked bus and fallen off a crashed rickshaw, I've pulled out the tooth of an ancient bicycle-wallah, fashioned homemade sanitary towels from rags and newspaper, and slept (perfectly innocently, I promise) with half a dozen teenage boys at the same time, possibly accidentally marrying at least two of them, also at the same time. On this basis, having my baby weighed on a rickety boat at the side of an oily, smelly river with a large and rapt audience does not constitute a problem.

For me.

I'm just not sure that the said baby will feel the same way.

Now, Simon has been travelling since he was five weeks old. He settles into aeroplanes like an old pro, doesn't care if it's forty degrees in the shade or minus five out of the immediate range of an open fire. He will snuggle up with me in the cocoon of a toddler-sized mosquito net (that's on the cards for tonight) and sleep for hours, and courtesy of baby-led weaning he will eat anything, the spicier the better, probably including cockerel crowns and fish larvae if I had a wont to let him taste them. Two things he doesn't do, however, are crawl – he sits on his bottom and turns around

11

in ever-increasing circles – and, more unusually, get weighed without making a squirming, squealing fuss. Hence, I don't weigh him very often, hence I don't know his weight, hence here we are right now. . .

I could try and explain this but life is too short. And anyway, Simon is looking, entranced, at the scales and thrusting out one pudgy hand to grab the shiny mechanism. So much so, that when Mr Nazrul leans over to pluck him out of my arms, crooning, 'baby, baby, how much you weight,' Simon doesn't bat an eyelid. Three seconds later, he's been plonked into the enormous measuring-dish and is sitting there looking like a placid but faintly astonished, and very white, Buddha. There's one in the eye for the baby clinic, then.

It's Mr Nazrul who looks as if he's about to cry. However many little brass weights he rapidly piles onto the opposing side, it doesn't yield. Soon he's run out and the only way he can get the scale to shift is to lean on it himself.

'Oh,' he says, disappointment all over his face. 'I don't weight your baby. I fail.'

I see the devilish tea being brought up the stairs and think on my feet. 'Don't give up so easily,' I tell him. 'You could measure him against a. . . a. . . bag of sugar. Or rice!' I admire my own resourcefulness, even as I wonder why I'm encouraging him. Oh yes, it's to avoid drinking the tea.

Fleetingly, I think of the story as it will sound in years to come; I left my baby sitting in the bowl of a giant weighing scales that had come from God-knows-where, just to avoid drinking a cup of tea. Alright, it's not like feeding him to crocodiles or leaving him outside the pub with a packet of crisps and a bottle of Coke... and, surely, nobody need ever remember this anyway... Except that they will; in the last few years Bangladesh has caught the tail-coat of the international technology boom and now even the poorest rickshaw driver has access to a cheap mobile phone. Judging from the cameras being held up around me, this will be on YouTube before we arrive on Bhola Island – our overnight destination.

'Baby is very fatty,' ruminates Mr Nazrul (I take this as a compliment; being fairly well-covered in Bangladesh is a sign that you are wealthy enough to eat good food and is something of an aspiration).

There is a lull in proceedings. Simon actually settles further into the weighing bowl, and attempts to get it to swing gently, before pausing, red faced and grunting, to fill his nappy – it looks like some kind of art installation, an experimental Tracey Emin/Anne Geddes collaboration.

The next thing I know, one of the crowd is proffering a water melon.

Simon is heavier than a medium-sized water melon.

Over the next few minutes, I learn he is also heavier than two medium-sized water melons, a brace of bananas, and probably three live chickens strung together by the feet, but we'll never be sure on that because the chickens won't sit still long enough to be measured.

'Apa, one more chance,' begs Mr Nazrul and I see it's a badge of honour for him now; he's come this far.

Simon still appears happy enough, probably thanks to the bucket of pomegranate seeds he's being fed by the delighted little boys who carried the scales, so I nod graciously.

Something is already being handed, over hand, over hand, from the quayside. It's a mammoth, sausage-shaped, greeny orange thing, and a football-crowd roar goes up as Simon and it fight for weight and they settle, neck and neck.

Balanced.

'This is how much is your baby!' Yells a triumphant Mr Nazrul.

How much is my baby?

Simon is the same weight as a large, unripe pumpkin.

The crowd cheers; I hold Simon aloft and Mr Nazrul does likewise with the pumpkin. I'm really getting into the spirit of the match, and then I see the astonished face of Ali peering at me from the back of the crowd. With as much decorum as I can muster, I bring Simon down to shoulder-level where he cuddles in happily. I sit down on my plastic chair and attempt to look like a respectable trustee of the orphanage we're on our way to visit and not the deranged showbiz mother of a child who has just won a bonny-baby contest at the fair. I bring myself to earth by calculating where best to attempt a nappy change.

With impeccable timing, the about-to-depart siren wails from the rear of the boat. I smile serenely at Ali, now at the front of the rapidly dispersing crowd – we might be entertaining but not enough for anyone to want to accompany us as far as Bhola – and leave Mr Nazrul to explain the game whilst I accidentally spill my cold cup of tea. Everyone is happy, and, extra result, Ali is soon the proud owner of a mutant pumpkin to take home to the children.

I have a sense of déjà vu two weeks later. At the much smaller Bhola ghat, an overloaded rowing boat, full of excited children, Simon included, takes us out into the river to await the seaplane back to Dhaka. The boat rocks alarmingly and my feet and ankles are wet. We bob alongside an intricate strand of fishing nets, all prepared for a heavy day's catch. After a few minutes, one of the loitering fishermen wades over. He is bare chested, his beard is tickling his naval and he has his lunghi fashioned into a pair of Speedo-sized shorts. He looks at Simon, looks me in the eye, and I know what is coming.

'How much is your baby?' he asks.

This time I am prepared. 'A large pumpkin,' I say proudly, and I take out the picture Ali has printed from his phone to prove it.

My face falls as the fisherman shakes his head.

'Yes, but, apa,' he says, 'how much is your baby weight in fishes. . .?'

Dear Gus

Rick Rutjens

Bali

Dear Gus.

It's difficult to imagine now that I didn't quite know what to do with you when you first arrived. Borne of travel, you'd been conceived in Bali during your mum's stint living and working on that island idyll. At your first trimester ultrasound, the doctor in Denpasar casually announced that you were 'viable'. Unable to comprehend that we did not want to know your gender, he'd argued with us before dismissing himself from the whole procedure with that one mechanical word. His offhandedness was so at odds with the breathless anxiety I felt at first glimpsing your growing form. Who would you be? Would I like you? Would you like me? Would I know what to do with you? Would I know how to be your dad?

Your first flight was in utero: Denpasar to Tullamarine. Tullamarine is a word that fascinated me from the first time I went there: to welcome Dutch relatives who had come to visit my father and his sprawling Catholic mob. As a kid I had assumed that 'tulla' meant air and when coupled with 'marine' that it was a take on the term 'airport'. It was actually the name of a nineteenth century Aboriginal prison-escapee-made-good. Anyho', you arrived at Tullamarine and I panicked. Not externally, but a deep internal panic. In fact, as your mother gestated you I nursed this unspeakable anxiety.

I had committed to build a house for your arrival, but it was not finished. There was a frame and a roof and walls and windows, but little beyond that. Your mother came to live with me at my parents' house in their spare room. It was an inauspicious beginning to our life together. My panic grew. This was not what I'd promised, nor what I'd hoped for. I knew not what to do with this woman who'd arrived into this tiny room seven months pregnant. I knew not what to do with the growing alarm I was feeling about your arrival. For the first time in my life I had dependants: it was not a moment of pride and burgeoning responsibility, it was a moment of terrifying, debilitating pressure.

I have heard since that it is instinctual to 'nest' prior to the arrival of the firstborn child. I nested with a vengeance. I hammered and nailed and screwed and glued and painted and fixed with a mania that channelled all the anxiety I was feeling and gave it a practical outlet. I became single-minded in my quest. I took my fear and turned it into energy: I finished the house fuelled on little but adrenalin. We moved in on February 13th. You were due on the 20th. Moving in did nought to relieve my anxiety though, in fact it made me realise that I had used building to avoid your mother, the claustrophobia of that little room and the inevitability of your arrival. If I could have disappeared in good conscience at that moment I would have.

You arrived at 6.23am on the 20th – right on time. It was a warm morning, the tapering end of a hot summer; a drought would be declared before the year was out. That morning it rained, though. As I cut your umbilical cord the first heavy drops fell outside the hospital windows, heralding the sort of shower that brings a sense of relief and a sweet smell of renewal from the parched earth. Two days later we brought you home to the house I had built for you.

As you read this you'll probably imagine that the rain is a metaphor: that your arrival heralded a sense of relief and renewal. It did not. Your arrival was the catalyst to the most difficult six months of my life. It wasn't your arrival actually; it was our reaction to your arrival. We didn't manage. We both tried to do what we thought was best but our instincts were askew, the black dog took a terrible hold and by the time you were reaching the half-year mark things were dire.

Then the phone call came from Bali. Would you come back? Your replacement has fallen through. We'll pay your fares, we'll accommodate and feed you. Yes, all three of you. In retrospect it may have been foolhardy, but at the time there was a straw and we clutched at it. Ten weeks in Bali. You, armed with your very own passport, flew back to where you'd been conceived.

I couldn't go for the whole time, so your mum's employer arranged a nanny for the first few weeks and your mum juggled work and breastfeeding. By the time I arrived the two of you had settled in to the upstairs rooms of a villa overlooking a rice paddy. The vista was constantly moving – storm clouds, ceremonial flags, chickens, farmers, ducks, banana leaves. You were happy. Your mum was not. Work on its own was an enormous undertaking, let alone trying to manage being a parent too. She had left Tullamarine exhausted and was now somewhere beyond that. I was frightened for her and for us.

For you and I, though, this was it. Out of that dire situation came this. This love. This selfless devotion. I think that this is what I had expected to feel when you were born, and I did to an extent, but this was more than that. This wasn't just an instinctual sense of protection of a vulnerable being, this was you and me as a team, a unit. This was you and me as two individuals inseparably connected by blood and circumstance.

We were together for almost every moment of your remaining time in Bali. We set your cot up in the second room and I slept in there with you so your mum could sleep through the night undisturbed. The three of us would breakfast on the balcony before sending your mum off to work on her scooter. You and I would then walk to the markets. We'd have coffee on the way and enter the markets from the back, away from the tourists. Everywhere we went the locals would stop and chat to you. Many of them knew your mum after her years living there, but many more simply wanted to get a smile from the blue-eyed, blonde-haired boy on my hip. You played up to all the attention, seeking out the gaze of those who were initially oblivious to you.

We spent our days walking, exploring, adventuring. To this day the thing we both love best is heading off on an adventure, whether that's trying to spot the kangaroos in our forest or a crazy road trip to Uluru and back or building a fort under the daybed or a week in the otherworldly glitziness of the Gold Coast and its theme parks. Being with you, having you as my other set of ears and eyes makes the world over anew for me. Things I would never do on my own are legitimised when I do them with you. You make me brave and joyously foolish and inquisitive and alive. What's down there, Dad? What does that taste like? What would happen if you mixed this with that? How do we grow crystals? What do we feed the tadpoles we caught? What's punk music? Can you play some for me? Every day is an adventure. Plans are made – sometimes carefully, often in haste – but how they eventually play out tends to be based on a series of whims, each one taking us a little further from our original intentions. Sometimes a trip to the supermarket for milk has us coming home hours later, our quest for the perfect playground or an icecreamery with liquorice icecream taking us away, away.

This letter seems to be taking as circuitous a route as some of our adventures – sorry, mister. Where was I? Ah, yes, Bali. We established a routine. Up early to the warm, bright days. Breakfast. Coffee. Market. Wander. Nap. Swim. Walk. Dinner. Bed. It was idyllic. Apart from the fact that your mum was feeling overwhelmed. While that cast a shadow over she and I, you were oblivious. You were making that joyful transition from infant to toddler: discovering that you had a body and that you could make it move; growing increasingly attentive to books and pictures and the world around you; understanding that a look or a smile from you could make someone happy; moving from breastmilk alone to solid foods... And that's where the market ladies come in. Rather than shop at ground level with the tourists we would venture down to the myriad stalls crammed into the lower sections of the market. There seemed to be nothing that couldn't be bought down there: fruit, vegetables, meat – both slaughtered and not – dried fish, chillies in more varieties than I have ever seen in one place, garlic too. There were animal parts I didn't recognise – although I didn't linger long at those stalls – herbs, spices, cooking implements, baskets, etcetera ad infinitum. Well, almost. The first morning we ventured down into this section of the market we were a novelty, tourists who'd lost their way. The second morning we got a smile or two. The third morning I could do little but watch for half an hour or so as you were passed from one smitten stallholder to another: the market ladies.

For weeks this became part of our morning routine. We'd get to the market and the ladies would have fruit bagged up and waiting for us – rambutans, mangoes, mangosteens, grapes, apples, oranges, tangerines, tangelos, lychees, pineapples, small, sweet bananas, huge pink passionfruit, jackfruit, papaya, longan. It seemed that we'd entered into some tacit agreement – they'd get to play with you, then they'd send us home with our day's supply of fruit. I always paid, although I was never sure how much what they'd bagged for us was worth. They would protest, waving the humidity-limp notes away – but would take them eventually. And so it was that your first solid food was not from me or your mother – it was from one of the market ladies. One would give you some exotic fruit or another and the rest would crowd around to watch your reaction. A good reaction and that fruit would be in our bag the next morning, a grimace and spit would see the offending fruit blackbanned – regardless of whether your mother or I would have actually liked it. Even now, all these years later, the thought of that time and those ladies makes me happy.

Bali was also where you learnt to love being in the water. We'd swim every afternoon – there was a pool attached to the villa. The Qantas staff had given you a rubber duck on your flight over: we could spend hours in the pool throwing and retrieving that duck. The swimming was always supervised by Nyoman, the nanny who had stayed on despite my arrival. She would gasp each time I threw you into the water, her tut-tut audible from where she sat on the balcony. Nyoman loved you. The times at the villa with her were delightful, her Balinese sense of calm cloaking all that she did. She'd potter during the day, sweep around the villa, chat to the locals who wandered by, practise her English by reading your books and asking me questions. She cried when it came time for us to return to the real world. There is still a photo of you and she in your bedroom. It is hard to imagine that the tiny cherub in that picture is the bike-riding, footy-kicking, swearing, funny, adventurous boy who lives with me now.

Occasionally prospective parents will ask me what it's like, being a dad. It's confounding, I say. If I wasn't your dad I doubt I'd want to be a dad. I fucking love being your dad! I love it like nothing else I have ever done. (Would you believe that I am crying as I type this. If this was a movie I'd be using a nibbed pen and an ink well and as I got to this part of the letter my tears would fall onto the page and blot the ink. . . Oh the clichés!) I feel as though you and I were somehow destined for one another. Of course I know that rationally what has happened is you were born and the person you are and will become is as a result of the fact that I am your dad – and that's what makes you special to me. In fact, now that I think about it it is actually some sort of cross-generational narcissism! That wasn't what I wanted to say though. What I wanted to say is that being your dad is actually a constant surprise, and that often that surprise is coupled inexorably with grief. Not a huge, mawing grief, just a nagging, niggling grief. A sadness that the person you'd been, the things that had marked you as being you – the idiosyncratic pronunciation of 'orange', the way you wanted to dance to Tojo over and over and over again – suddenly just stop. And then you're onto the next thing, the next iteration of you. One morning recently we were looking at the tadpoles and wrigglers in the pond and you remarked that both started their lives as one thing and ended it as another. You asked if many animals did this. And at that moment I thought, yes, mister – and you're one of them. There have been dozens of you over the years since your birth. Each one growing out of the one before, each one bringing both surprise and that petite grief that always catches me off-guard.

You're at your mum's house tonight and I miss you. I sat in your room on your bed and glanced around. I spotted the photo of you and Nyoman and thought back to that time, that you. And I wanted you to know that I'm not scared anymore. I know who you are: you are you. I know I like you. I know you like me. I still don't really know what to do, but I do know now that making it up as I go along is ok. I know how to be your dad – by loving you.

I do love you.

Dad. x

Edinburgh to Brest

Sylvain Morisot

France

Here we are sitting on the train from Edinburgh bound for London, with two more trains still to catch: London to Paris, then Paris to Brest, Brittany.

As I sit in the seat, Isabella in her mother's lap, I realise she is craving for food, silly me for not noticing it has already been two hours since her last feed. You would think that by now something easy would exist to make bottle preparation easier, instead here I am pouring hot burning water from my thermos to the bottle stuck between my legs, making sure I don't spill any bit outside the bottle. Now the easy part pouring the powdered milk into the bottle. Yeah hey, ha – no wait, I need to find a way to cool it down now. Isa is now eyeing me with interest as she gets more and more hungry.

Finding myself in the toilet to cool down the bottle only to realise that it is hot water that comes out, well done boy. Then I feel cold on my arm; someone just opened the window in the in-between carriage space. Here you go, bottle cooled down in 4 minutes thanks to a 200km/h wind-flowing from the window.

The rest of the trip to London now looks easy.

With the train finally arriving in London, we manage to gather our luggage and to make it to London's top modern Saint Pancras station. One of the good things is its changing facilities, you can fit two people with big luggage in it, making the nappy change a walk in the park.

Time for a coffee to get our senses back on track and then we are rolling from London to Paris for two and half hours. TGVs. . . nice train but you can't open windows on these ones, so back to square one on going halfway through the train to the bar to get a glass of water with ice to cool down Isa's milk and to get more coffee. By now it has already been a long day and I am flying on auto-pilot.

Ha Paris, city of love but not of travel with babies as we will soon find out. Sitting on the metro and trying not to die from overheat, they could use a good air-con in there, I am watching Isa struggle with the noise and smell that is going around her. She has seen so much, heard so much in less than twelve hours, I really wonder how she will cope tonight spending the night in Paris before heading to Brest tomorrow morning. My other half, Nadia, looks like she has spent a week without sleep and is sending me angry looks about being in the metro rather than a taxi. I will pay for that one later, I am sure.

Finally we arrive, at least most people gave Isa a good smile that she gives back, little creature she is.

I must say I was a bit afraid about the hotel, will there be a kettle to get boiled water for the bottle? Will the sink of the bathroom be big enough to put all the stuff we need to sterilize? Entering the room I can feel the stress going away, a kettle sits on the table and after crossing over the bed I can see a deep large sink. We are ready for the night.

Meanwhile, hunger is starting for Nadia and I, which means it is time to nose out a baby friendly restaurant in Paris, that's where the real fun starts. After a brief re-con of the surrounding area, including a look at the train station nearby for tomorrow's train, we decide it is a lost cause and go for some sushi & beer takeaway to have in our room. We are after all, in the beginning of June 2014 and the football World Cup has every bar full to their heads.

Having bought a magical travel cot that folds itself to the size of a large Frisbee, we set Isabella down for the night and start to relax a bit and to enjoy the food and beer. Sleep will come with no extra time.

Waking up to sun and the sounds of the irritated Parisian commuters, Isa's cry sounded almost delightful compared to the rest. It has been the fastest packup we have managed so far. Despite having almost a full spare hour before the train leaves, we are still glad we took the hotel five minutes from the train station.

It has been a long time since I took a TGV and what a surprise, five star changing facilities. The two of us plus the baby fit, so it is nice and practical. A good start to our trip.

Isa attracts every grandmother on the train, some more chatty than others. Overall a good, not eventful trip of four and a half hours, and I even managed to get a power nap.

I can smell the ocean before the train even stops, I know that sensation, having spent 4 years in Brest. It feels good to be back. First stop, car rental office, which does not have any baby seats of course. Luckily we knew that in advance and got a friend to meet us with her sister's ten year old car seat. The drive to her home was easy, with the baby sleeping through the many curves of the Brittany countryside.

My friend Muriel, Mumu for those who know her well, has an old house by the seaside inherited from her grandmother. Most of the second floor is still to be refurbished, but it is usable for guests.

Ho yes, it was June, but nights were really cold, so the baby goes to her magic cot with extra layers, which of course she does not like. The changing station was on the bed in the next room. I must say I should have known it was going to be freezing for the night feed but still I was a bit surprised the first time, brrrrrrr.

Our first day was made up of crepes by the seaside in the middle of the legendary Meneham rock structure. The main challenge was yet again changing the baby, with no changing rooms available. Challenges the next day were on a different level. First time on a boat for the baby, is she gonna be sick? Or is she going to enjoy the ride? Well guess what? She slept the 15 minutes it took to go to the island. For the trip we went for the baby carrier as a pram would have been a disaster to get on the boat. The visit was nice and the baby finally got her eyes open to see the surroundings. By now our skills in getting milk cooled down to perfection at the right time had improved a lot, like a barista finally mastering the latte art. After boating and island hopping a nice cafe was more than a necessity. And surprise, we find our first French cafe with a changing room, play space for kids, and good coffee. The trip back saw us changing the baby on the boot of the car as we were half way back to the house.

Now being just a hundred meters away from the beach does have its uses – like going bare foot over there. The sea was a wee bit cold I must say, but I could see in Isa's half closed eyes that she is desperate to touch this new blue thing that is coming back and forth. She is also quite puzzled by the yellow surface that looks smooth, so here we remove our socks and pull up leggings to give Isa her first sea and sand trial.

The touch down on the sand was unexpected for Isa and she tried to get her footing, but only managed to dig her feet into the wet sand. Hum what's that? Ha, I see her start to enjoy that wet feeling of the sand, but wait something is coming fast at her back. . . splash! First wee wave, knee high. A blank face is the only thing we will get out of it, but it was quite a good first and she will soon be ready for surfing.

While giving Isa her night bottle in the attic-like room I realise I am really looking forward to being at my parents' home in a few days, and to be given a rest and be able to sleep til lunch, ho yes we will.

The trip back from Brest to the Champagne area where my parents live should have been easy, except that there are train strikes the very same day we are supposed to leave. And having a baby does not make it easier to find alternative seats for cancelled trains. Anyway, welcome to France by the way, the local train was ill equipped for baby and we ended up changing Isa on the floor of the train with half the people not happy about the smell. Yeah, formula milk bottle poo is indeed the best. Perhaps we should have thought of that to get extra space in the train. Next time.

Home finally, ha, I can already feel the real holiday starting, dinner is already ready, my mum is playing with Isa and

Nadia and I can have a drink outside on the warm late June evening. While sitting outside we finally have some time to reflect how easily Isa has coped with all the changes she has been through in the last 13 days. She has seen so many people, in train stations, trains, subway; and even the changes in scenery, going from a British cottage to huge rocks by the beach and now nice green grass full of new things to discover. If I think about it now I think it might be one of the reasons she is so easygoing with new people.

Ok Isa, time for bed now, you will see grandma in the morning, early. . . well what can I say my mum is an early bird and so is Isa so the logical step is to let them play together at 6.30am and for me to get back to bed while it is still warm and my is head still sleepy. I think that is the best part of having your parents around, they can help a lot in getting back those lost sleeping hours. And we have the best night's sleep since baby was born – if we consider the night starting from 6.30 in the morning and ending up at noon.

Tonight is a big party for Isa, BBQ with all the family, so about 20 new faces to memorise for her. But before that it is pool time. . . in a big bucket. Yeah, the advantage of being a baby is that you can fit in something pretty small. So, big bucket of water it is and that nice swimming gear we bought for the occasion. I have to admit I am going to use these pictures as blackmail when she is fifteen years old and does not want to listen to us.

Having so many people requires a good old French drink, Marquise de champagne to accommodate the guests. Isa is in a nice white dress that seems to puzzle her, and here we go, with the hand the baby over to your neighbour game. Isa is playing well, giving her best behaviour to people and receiving so many gifts that we don't know how we are going to get them back to Edinburgh.

At that moment seeing all my family around Isa I just knew we would have to do it again next year as everyone enjoyed it, or maybe the Marquise had a bit to do with that. The night goes fast when you wake up a lot and again I am so thankful to pass on the ball in the morning to my mum. Yes, we fully intend to make this visit to my parents count. It is a win win, we rest and they get to play with Isa as much as they can, not a bad deal, I must say.

Well hello, birds and sunshine, it is morning and we are still in bed. Isa is playing like mad with grandma and grandpa and they love it. I must say I was a bit afraid about how much they would remember from their days as early parents and if they would still know how to change nappies. They were a bit rusty on the nappy changing, but they had not lost any of their parenting skills. And Isa is so easy on them.

I am preparing a surprise for Isa this afternoon, a trip to the vegetable garden next to the house. Which turns out to be one of the best ideas of the day, we sit her in between tomato rows and carrots. I doubt she will ever remember it, but she enjoyed the touch of the leaves and the soil.

So much to see and already we are moving to our next place on the map, the mountains. The place we go to ski during winter is also open during summer and it is nice, green trees everywhere. Unfortunately Isa is not going to sleep much, I think, because she slept for the most part of the 5 hours drive, damn I forgot how good cars were at making babies sleep easily. My bad for next time.

Ha, breakfast on the terrace with views over the mountains and Isa watching the butterflies everywhere and also the bees. Now I don't mind bees, but I would hate to have to go to the hospital because Isa gets bitten by a bee. So lets try not to hug the bees Isa, ok?

This afternoon it is quick road trip to Annecy, a beautiful town by a lake at the foot of a mountain. It is like a small Venice. First advice, don't go there with a pram. Knowing this, I choose to go with the baby carrier. It was a judicious choice. The streets are very narrow and it can be pretty busy, but how nice it is. Isa is looking everywhere as everywhere is different.

We walk and walk and then it is time for everyone to feel a bit thirsty. And here comes the fun, finding a bar/cafe to have a drink where people are not annoyed at having a baby around. Finally we find one, order some drinks from the "can't be bothered" waiter, then it is time to make Isa's milk, and of course nowhere can we find the waiter to ask for a bowl of cold water. So plan B in action and it is back to toilet time. Yeah, good luck with that, there is only one toilet and it is tiny and there is a queue. Well, the person behind me is going to wait for quite some time when it is my turn, a bottle of milk does not cool down in two minutes. Luckily for everyone by the time it is my turn Nadia manages to get hold of the waiter and we have a glass just big enough to put the bottom of the bottle into.

Oh and of course there are no changing facilities. Remember that if you go to historical towns in France; cafes or restaurants with changing facilities are very few. Thankfully there is a huge park going all along the one side of the Lake so it is nappy change in the park time, Isa seems to like it a lot.

All in all it was quite a good day, baby was nice and easy, except that she is now pretty tired and is making our life miserable in the car on the way back. Hopefully she will be tired and going to sleep well. . . says the man who will wake up fifteen times in the coming night.

The next day was simply uneventful. . . till the evening. Dress up time for pictures as the game on TV tonight is France v Argentina in the World Cup. Isa has a nice 50% French 50% Argentina body shirt and is diving for an imaginary ball like a goalkeeper in between her mom in Argentinian t-shirt and me with a half blue, half red t-shirt and a full white t-shirt to make a mock-up of the French flag.

The few days in the mountains were fun and we saw quite a few advantages and disadvantages to living in France with a baby. Edinburgh is definitely a lot more baby friendly than any town in France so far.

Going back to Edinburgh we stopped for a night in Paris again and the idea was to see as many friends as possible on the Saturday morning for a breakfast, before our train to London at noon. Let's say we got sun burned, as we found a nice terrace with croissants and good coffee. Everybody was all sweet on Isa and she gave it back pretty well with her good smile and talking. The return was good but really felt long this time. I believe it is the last time we will travel home by train for a while. Christmas will be by plane, no questions.

Looking back on the trip I can see that travelling with little monsters is very good for them, to open their eyes and senses; however it is tiring and needs to be thought through carefully. Also it makes me happy to live in Scotland as it is, so far as I have experienced it, a lot more baby friendly than France.

First Class Compartment

Sarah Dyer

Singapore

I arrived in Singapore the month before my baby's due date. At that time I lived in a suburb of Jakarta, Indonesia's chaotic capital. For the birth it was generally accepted to go to Singapore or return to one's country of origin, in my case the UK. Singapore was closer, I'd lived there before and it meant a quicker return to a normal home life in Jakarta. Also, it meant my husband would have a better chance to be at the birth.

I arrived alone, armed with the necessary mountain of paperwork to enter the country. Paperwork giving proof I was fit to travel and several tomes of agreement to not make any claims to Singaporean nationality for my baby.

This was the most important journey of my life. I was excited yet calm at having got this far in the pregnancy after a few years of epic fails in the baby-making department.

Shortly after marrying, whilst living in Singapore, I had become pregnant but it was ectopic. The foetus had attached inside the fallopian tube which then ruptured as the foetus grew. Sometime during the emergency procedure, I awoke from the anesthetic but unable to convey this to the surgery team, they continued cutting into me until it was noticed. An experience that was almost topped (but not quite) by the gynaecologist making me watch the video of the procedure in order that I didn't harbour thoughts that I was still pregnant. 'See? Baby gone,' she said.

Six unsuccessful months on a fertility drug, a disastrous womb x-ray ('Why won't the dye go into your right fallopian tube?' the practitioner asked pushing at my womb impatiently as if it was somehow my fault. 'Because it was removed,' I replied. This information was not in his notes) and an accusation from the doctor's receptionist that I couldn't be doing it right, I should be pregnant by now, made me realise I needed different, perhaps kinder help.

After some research I found the doctor in Singapore who was to become central to my quest to have a baby. Soon I had a positive pregnancy test that lasted a couple of days but followed this with a D & C (a procedure usually reserved for terminating pregnancies) to give my womb a 'bit of a spring clean', then another procedure to deal with polyps. I'm no longer certain of the amount of surgical procedures I had.

My husband's job moved from Singapore to Jakarta so I did too; a positive step to move on from all the anguish. Once the dust settled (for dust read: house hunting/nest building, making new friends, moving and unpacking shipment, usually around four to six months) and the century turned, I booked the IVF treatment at a reputable fertility centre in Jakarta.

As I arrived for the first appointment on the correct day of my cycle however, the specialist calmly stated he could not get the blood test results quick enough to act on them for the IVF. It was a crushing blow.

IVF is not a blasé treatment with guaranteed success, as often portrayed by the British media. It is a last ditch attempt to grow your own baby in your womb.

Even if you produce lots of eggs and they all become fertilised, there are no guarantees that a pregnancy will follow or that any pregnancy will last to term. It is also a highly invasive procedure; your body is forced into menopause then both ovaries are jump-started. Having more than one egg ripen at once is painful.

All mature eggs are then collected; any visions of fluffy hens, soft straw and warm eggs must immediately be dispelled. This is done with or without a general anesthetic depending on the clinic.

Your partner must shoot his load into a jar to hand over to the lab. His sperm may be tested and the best mixed or even injected into the eggs.

After a few days and more drugs you might be ready as receptacle to receive the eggs into your womb. Again, not the sexiest way to conceive, but hey! You are desperate.

So, the journey so far had not been smooth; I was sitting alone (husband on business in France) receiving the news that this specialist could or would not help. From being optimistic, determined and excited, I became a burst and flaccid balloon. If I didn't have the help of a specialist, how could I ever hope to have a child? I telephoned my doctor in

Singapore who spoke to the local health clinic near my house. We would DIY the IVF.

Over the next few weeks I drove (or rather I was driven, but that sounds too posh for my fourth-hand push-me-pull-you camper van) around Jakarta's bumpy streets sourcing the right drugs and needles. When I couldn't find any more, strangers carried them as hand-luggage from Singapore and I am forever grateful for their kindness, they will never know how much it meant.

My friend, a nurse in her pre-expat life, taught me to self-inject so as not to have to visit the clinic each day and to be in control of my own treatment. I flew to Singapore for the egg retrieval, alone but with friends there it was enjoyable, if a little tense. I couldn't bring myself to drink more than a glass of wine even though I was reminded of the many tales of conception on debaucherous nights. Relax, they said.

I bought a pack of ten cigarettes and a lighter and kept them in my bag in case it really did get too much. I still have that lighter.

My husband joined me for the last few crucial days. With the little pot of sperm nestling at body temperature in my bra we drove to the hospital to introduce them to my eggs, all three of them. Through the ICSI injection process, a couple of days later I was told two of the eggs had fertilised and they would be popped into my womb.

I spread my legs for another team of strangers and breathed those little bundles of hope into touch. I really did have all my eggs in one basket. My last chance at growing my own.

We returned to Jakarta to wait out the two weeks before taking a pregnancy test. My husband went to work as normal. 'There's nothing we can do now,' he said. But he was wrong. Each day was marked by promises to those potential lives, filled with love, pacts made with every imaginable god, wished-for scenarios filled with bubbling baby laughter.

I ate a lot of crisps. I couldn't make plans in the real world, my life was on hold until I knew one way or another. My mother in law was her usual positive self: 'Well, it might not work,' she said. 'You've got to think of that.' No, I don't.

It was out of my hands and into my heart. I had done everything possible to help a baby into existence and now it was nature's game of chance. Choose me!

I didn't dare breathe when I did the test, but there it was, the thin blue line over which I'd crossed into the realm of almost-motherhood. It was still a possibility that the little ball of cells may have turned left and, rather than ending up in first class, may yet be stuck in the remaining fallopian tube.

I booked a scan as soon as possible at the local clinic. There it was, the little throbbing blob of my baby, the rapid ping-ping-ping of its newly-formed heartbeat, in a perfectly safe place, in my womb, a part of me and alive. My husband's lack of excitement was understandable; we'd thought things were going well before and then it had all gone Pete Tong. He was trying to keep an even keel. But for me, this baby was my sanity.

The two years since the ectopic had been filled with monthly heartbreak for me; two weeks of excitement to ovulation then two weeks of hope until my period mocked the person I wanted to be. Friends regularly shared their joy at becoming pregnant, unaware of my hidden grief. I was truly happy for them but I cried in the loos of all the best homes and hotels of Jakarta, plus a fair few in the UK too. Now I could be happy for myself.

There was no way I would let this baby go. Some mid-pregnancy bleeding couldn't quash my determination, even when the doctor advised bed rest to 'let nature take its course.'

My belly swelled and I quite literally blossomed. Home leave in the UK was filled with sunny days and a love affair with soft fruit and peas in their pods.

At seven and a half months pregnant I was so full of energy I organised an art exhibition for a friend, designing the layout and co-ordinating the opening night which raised funds for charity, all in lieu of painting the baby's room. Then it was time to leave for Singapore with my baby safe and almost ready to come out.

There, I went shopping to my heart's content; gathering the necessities and many un-necessities for my first-born, filling the spaces in between with visits to various food stalls and reacquainting myself with old, tasty friends and drinking lots of coconut water straight from green coconuts.

I walked out each morning (in itself a joy, since walking around Jakarta was just not an option) after a hearty breakfast from the Goodwood Park Hotel's international buffet. International buffets are designed specifically for pregnant women; everything you could ever wish to eat in exactly the quantities to satisfy needs. Full English this morning? How would you like your eggs ma'am? Just one prawn dumpling with your nasi lemak? Help yourself. Rice porridge with dried fish followed by oat porridge and honey? Whatever you want. The Dutch Ambassador's wife marveled at my inventive combinations, though she may have been exercising her famous diplomacy.

The short walks between shopping malls gave me enough of an appetite to indulge in my favourite Singapore dish, ever: Hainanese Chicken Rice. Choose between dark or pale skin (dark every time thanks) boiled chicken which is served with delicately flavoured (with ginger, garlic and chicken stock) fluffy rice, black sauce, a fiery sambal and garnished with icy cucumber and fragrant coriander with a sprinkling of sesame oil. This is heaven on a plate.

Next door to the Goodwood Park Hotel is an older mall called Far East Plaza. On the fifth floor is a small food shop called Hainanese Delicacy Chicken Rice. With a bowl of the nurturing chicken broth on the side, along with a plate of crunchy greens, I could eat this every day of my life.

I was forced to learn to cook it for myself later living in Aberdeen, but no matter how many times I make it, it will never be as good as that shop's.

Once the ridiculously dramatic episode (a clear reflection of all my attempts at having a baby – an emergency caesarian section because the umbilical cord was wrapped around his neck, twice) of my son's birth was out of the way, the first place he visited after returning to the hotel's serviced apartment from the hospital was the Hainanese Delicacy Chicken Rice stall. After all, I had been a long five days without it.

With hindsight, perhaps I could have ordered a daily delivery, a tiffin box full of delicious nurturing delight, but it rather slipped my mind. You see, I had this funny wee man whom I couldn't seem to put down long enough for me to think about chicken. Or rice. I came to my senses though (the drugs wore off) and my appetite returned.

When my well-traveled baby was ten years old, I took him back to Singapore. His frequent concern as he grew was 'Where do I belong?' As a 'third culture child' he questioned what he was in terms of nationality. He holds a British passport but if he chooses to become 'international mobile' (always makes me think of Thunderbirds for some reason), any child he has with his partner will not be guaranteed British citizenship unless born in the UK. His parents are Welsh and English; he has spent the majority of his life in Scotland. Yet he identifies with Singapore as his birthplace.

We walked the older, narrow streets of Katong on the East Coast of Singapore where I once lived. We ate at open fronted shop houses, sat on once-white plastic chairs. I was working my way through memories, my boy was discovering for the first time.

For our second week, we moved to the Goodwood Park Hotel; within Singapore's ever changing, always progressing centre, though somehow it remained exactly as I remembered. Except the breakfast, which had downsized considerably.

But it didn't matter. For next door, same as ever, was Far East Plaza and with unfathomable excitement I rode the escalators to the top floor. There it was. Hainanese Delicacy Chicken Rice. Heaven in a single-fronted unit. It was like a pilgrimage to the high altar of chicken rice (disclaimer: though many Singaporeans will disagree as matters of the best chicken rice in town are hotly and frequently debated, this place will remain my favourite among all the stalls I've visited) and we squeezed through the narrow shop to some spare seats at the back. No menu. Just choose between pale or dark skin; greens or no greens.

Within minutes set before us were two plates of moist chicken with perfect white mounds of rice, two bowls of glistening broth. There sat the small dishes of fiery red sambal and sweet black sauce. I took time to inhale the fragrant steam as if to ground my senses in the reality of where I was and with whom.

I closed my eyes and when I opened them my son was already half way through his. 'Oh my god, this is amazing,' he said, though he didn't stop eating. For the remainder of that week we went back almost every day he loved it so.

Another day we met with the doctor who had helped to conceive my son. It was as though I wanted to show him I could indeed look after such a precious gift. The doctor gets a lot of that but he doesn't seem to tire of the joy.

My son was a week old when he posed for his first passport picture. Still crinkly and new, his little fists clenched and tight to his face, eyes demanding attention from the camera lens. His first passport picture for his first passport and his first unattached journey. My baby, with all those miles to his name even before he was conceived. Platitudinous statements about the years flying by become reality: now my son talks about making journeys by himself. To France for a cultural exchange, even to Venezuela to visit a friend. His travels with me are coming to an end as I set him free to find his own way.

My own journey has changed direction too, and I prepare by unpacking metaphorical baggage to travel light.

Finding Our Bearings on the Banks Peninsula

Meghan J. Ward

New Zealand

'**W**e are so, so close,' I reassure my ten-month-old as we round the final hilltop that hides the ocean beyond this stretch of road on New Zealand's South Island. When we crest the highest point my spirits lift a little. Far down below the undulating hills of the Banks Peninsula, a sea of blue meets the barren hillsides with a fringe of white caps crashing ashore. But, Mistaya doesn't care about the beauty. After 27 hours of travel from our home in Canada to Christchurch, she is blowing a gasket, and we're barely hanging on ourselves.

Plagued with a raging migraine and motion sickness from the endlessly winding roads, the reassurance is equally intended for me. Curling up on the roadside looks more appealing than continuing, but we are just minutes away from our accommodation for the night in Akaroa. I switch to the driver's seat to ease the dizziness, and promptly realize I have chosen the lesser of two evils. Cars speed towards me in the right-hand lane, the one I am accustomed to driving in, and the windshield wipers start whenever I hit the blinker.

Finally, we descend the coastline in a zigzag of switchbacks that match those from the ascent. The baby wails in her car seat as we round one 'final' corner, then one more. As fate would have it, we can't find the holiday park we'd booked for the night. And as luck would have it, we never made a deposit, so we find the nearest coffee shop, hop online, and book a different one – thirteen kilometers back.

The room is finally quiet. Cries have subsided and transitioned to the soft, rhythmic whistle of a baby soundly sleeping. I can't tell if my husband, Paul, is asleep on the bottom bunk. Desperately tired, I lay awake coming to grips with the fact that we are concluding the first day of a 70-day adventure through the South Pacific. My thoughts are interrupted as the New Zealand skies over this eastern coastline unleash a hailstorm, and ice pellets pound the roof of our cabin. *Surely the little one will wake up.* She doesn't, and I breathe a sigh of relief.

Exhausted and weary, I stare up at corrugated tiles on the ceiling, counting them as I think through the trip ahead. We have travelled this way before, filling trips to the brim with ambitious goals and jam-packed schedules that were borderline insane. *We are seasoned travellers, right?* As a couple we have hopped islands in the Caribbean, trekked in the Himalaya, and skied in the Arctic. Solo trips have taken us to adventure-filled destinations like Ethiopia, Vanuatu and Costa Rica.

As experienced travellers, our itinerary seemed full, but feasible: four countries, seventeen flights. . . only one baby.

We aren't being naïve, we thought. Mistaya has already joined us on travels throughout Canada, and on long hikes back at home in Alberta, in the backcountry of Banff National Park. We knew a baby would change the way we'd travel and how her needs would have to come first. We knew we'd have to pull over for roadside diaper changes or nursing sessions, look for an impromptu hike when naptime came calling, and change our already loose plans on a whim.

What we didn't know was that travel with a baby would turn our lives completely upside-down; that at the same time we'd experience our highest of highs and lowest of lows, utter misery and complete joy.

What we didn't know was that we'd come home feeling like we'd run a marathon seventy days in a row.

Our second day begins at 2 a.m. It is 6 a.m. back at home, and Mistaya doesn't understand that the time change actually *gains* us four more hours sleep. I look over at Paul, who is sitting in his underwear, half-awake, cutting grapes into quarters. The situation is desperately funny, and all I can do is crack a joke to relieve the overwhelming sense of doom that lingers in the air. *We will get through this*, I tell myself. *We'll find our groove again. This is only the second day.*

We have six hours to wait until the first restaurant opens near the docks in Akaroa. Six hours to survive the interminable challenge of 'killing time' with a baby. We play with stacking cups on the bed for thirty-six seconds, read a book for seven, and set a record at twelve minutes of play in the camp kitchen. We do it over and over until it's time to leave.

Growing impatient, we depart early for a walk along the water, placing Mistaya on Paul's back in a soft carrier. This is our favourite way to explore the world with her. Being hands-free feels like the ultimate freedom as we walk down the short pier of this historic town and stare out at the sea. The early-morning air of late New Zealand summer is cool, but a welcome change from the winter chill back home.

I breathe in the freshness and it gives me a moment of clarity, only to realize how uncertain I feel about this trip. We are explorers without a compass, treasure hunters without a map, arrows without a target.

We have lost our bearings – as people, parents, travellers.

After breakfast we walk along the water again. Orange kayaks tied to nearby docks rise and fall and thump each other gently as waves make their way to the shore. We are treated to blue sky and sunshine on our first morning on the Banks Peninsula. My eyes drift across the bay of sailboats to the green hills on the other side, then out to the ocean. Coming from Banff, a town surrounded by mountains, it feels odd to see the uninterrupted line of the horizon. Its boundlessness excites my spirit, and for a minute I consider the adventures to come on this trip. For a minute I see the bigger picture: that our moment-by-moment challenges are just drops of water in the colossal ocean.

I'm snapped back to the present by the gleeful chatter of my little girl standing between my legs. 'Bir!,' she exclaims, not quite sounding the 'd' as she points to seagulls pecking at the earth nearby. Then, crouching low to the ground, she picks up a handful of pebbles and releases them. Moving my gaze from the endless stretches of the sea to the child at my feet, I crouch down and transfer more pebbles into her tiny palms. 'Bir!,' she exclaims once more, scattering the rocks. Her father scoops her up in his arms, and they chase the birds along the shoreline until it's time to gather pebbles once more.

Then, it hits me. The only thing anchoring us, the only point of reference in a vast unknown, is the very person who is throwing everything off course. There is nothing we can do but surrender and let Mistaya lead.

Despite our exhaustion, we take the day to explore, driving the peninsula's Summit Road to gain views of the neighbouring bays. Our emotions waffle like the road that snakes its way back and forth along the highlands, skirting bluffs that drop precariously towards the sea. We stop for cheerful play at a picnic area, then endure ceaseless crying when Mistaya boasts her most improbable of talents: the inability to fall asleep in the car when she is most tired.

In these moments of unrelenting whining, no amount of parenting or travel experience can save us.

Hope eventually returns, and offers respite. Accepting the situation is a good antidote. For a second night I can't sleep, so I step out into the darkness to look up at the sky and take comfort in the stars. The simple act of stargazing has carried me through many uncertain moments in life. It assuages the soul, whether home in the Rockies or when my wanderlust has taken me elsewhere. When the internal landscape is more unfamiliar than the external, staring at the heavens grounds me on both accounts.

The skies over the Banks Peninsula are pitch black and flecked with stars, the Milky Way streaking from horizon-to-horizon. I let out a contented sigh, then bend my neck to the side, as far as it allows. This is my first time in the Southern Hemisphere, and tonight when I look up, I take one glance at Orion and let out a laugh, then smile. The great hunter and his conspicuous belt are hanging upside-down, like he's lost his bearings in the sea of stars.

Orion reminds me – perhaps teases me – to let go. To stop trying to find something familiar. To settle into the unknown, into the adventures that travel with a baby brings. To accept the exhaustion, the tough times, the tears. To get lost with curiosity, chase the seagulls, pick up pebbles.

If the stars can hang upside-down and still cling to the sky, surely I can hang on, too.

Trading Places

Stuart A . Patterson

For Bonita Ariadne Jordan

Turkey, Malta, Spain & Greece had browned
Your skin to a passport of possibles.
In your eyes was another of my kind
Never met yet always, somehow, around.

Blu-Tacking *Ten Colour Views Of Patmos*
To your bedroom wall, you'd clamber onto my knee,
All lisp & lovely, exotically three
Years old, poster child for another's loss.

That party trick of counting to ten
In Spanish amazed the shop-keeper
We sometimes met in the village;
A warning shot of the unknown to men.

While you were peeing in the blue & purest
Seas or cutting small swathes in Amsterdam,
I packed a bag for tropical Arran,
Spent the summer cooking fry-ups for tourists.

Taking my large hand into the confidence
Of your own, tanned, tiny, always leading,
A day trip to Largs on a jolting bus
Felt like a very first crossing of continents,

Or scaling the heights of the breakwater
Bordering Troon in squally winter storms,
Brow against the universe, dragging me
Into the teeth of the gale, & the future.

I carry these memories now as I used
To carry you shoulder-high through years
Where memory lasted the happy length
Of an outing, a bus trip, a new pair of shoes.

Winter Weekend on the West Coast

Sophie Isaacson

Scotland

Sitting out on deck with my baby on my lap I took a deep breath of sea air and looked across the ocean. My belly fluttered, full of excitement as I took in the endless horizon and considered the undiscovered world which awaited us. I held him near as the cold salty breeze whipped around us, I knew that this tiny adventure would be the first of many.

I drove off the ferry, weary from a four hour journey with an eight week old baby who had no intentions of drifting off to sleep. We were headed for a weekend at Barcaldine Farm, near the fishing town of Oban. The November evening was closing in as I picked up a few supplies and set off along the road. The farm was easy to find and the bumpy track along to the house was a perfectly slow and hilarious way to build up my anticipation as the farm bounced closer and closer to us through the fading dusk light.

As I got out of the car a smell of manure crept up my nose, I smiled, this was just what I'd been hoping for. I knocked on the big wooden door and within seconds we were greeted by our beautiful hostess, Jane. As we were shown to our room I instantly felt at home in the farmhouse. The warm kitchen, obviously the heart of the house, boasted a fire engine red Aga and a huge table and chairs, ready for us to sit at and have dinner. The smell of roasting lamb wafted through the house and my belly grumbled noisily! Our room was upstairs and had its own fireplace. The wallpaper was floral, busy, blue and on every wall, but I liked the vintage look of the room and felt like we'd been transported into a scene from Downton Abbey!

After feeding baby Teddy and wrapping him up in his blanket I headed down for dinner. I was handed a generous glass of white wine and served a hearty plate of delicious, juicy lamb and local vegetables. The conversation flowed easily and I felt perfectly relaxed, warm and full of wholesome home cooking.

The next three days were a magical blur of walks around the stunning farm grounds. We helped to feed the two calves, Amelie and Alice, their lunch, brushed the manes of the fluffy Icelandic ponies and threw sticks for the playful collie dog, Bramble.

Baby Teddy was more relaxed than ever, he had lots of naps and especially loved walking through the forest staring up at the branches waving and swaying in the breeze. I felt inspired by the beauty of the landscape and spent the afternoons writing and sketching from our bedroom window as baby Teddy slept in his travel cot.

Each meal produced from the Aga was more delightful than the last and our hostess bent over backwards to make Teddy and I feel completely at home. It was a weekend of calm relaxation where I had the chance to really focus on baby Teddy. I'll never forget those blissful days snuggling in that beautiful old farm bedroom with my tiny boy gazing up at me.

Escaping for a few days with your baby is a really good way to forget about the bustle of everyday chores and visits from neighbors. I loved having the time to walk at leisure around the farm with Teddy and the long mornings free from haste where we sat in bed together sipping tea and catching up on episodes of New Girl. I have a feeling that I'll treasure the memory of those three days for the rest of my life.

The Long Short-Haul

Nicky Torode

Gatwick to Guernsey

You won't remember this, I said showing my 5 year old an old photo of us which had just fallen out of a travel book. How could you, I continued, you were only 9 months old and although you were not yet ready to put your tiny booted feet forward into the wide world, you were already boarding your first flight.

We're going on a plane just like your joey toy plane, I had mimed with my arms outstretched. My fear, I vividly remember now, was creeping up on me and starting to project itself. The photo, though, showed me looking strangely relaxed. On boarding the plane I recall how I was anticipating a bawling, inconsolable baby, exacerbated by hard Paddington stares from fellow passengers.

Armed with all your favourite toys, your least disturbing rattle, wind up melody player and baby food pots galore, I sat you on my lap and struggled to fit your seat belt onto mine. Seriously, with all the technology in the world why hadn't they yet invented something reassuringly safer than a strap, ill fittingly clipped onto my seat belt?

The air stewardess went through all the usual air safety procedures for what seemed like an achingly long time. You watched mesmerised. Pointing your chubby little fingers at her and smiling and dribbling back at me. Perfect! This stewardess had become an ally in my battle for peace. I started wishing she would become the in-flight entertainment! I could pay her, I thought, and let out a squeal of disbelief at my own crazy thoughts.

So far, so good. Your beaming smile gave me momentary relief as you were now fascinated by the sick bag you'd pulled from the seat pocket in front.

Dummy in, and mummy breathing purposeful deep breaths, we eventually took off. Good boy, I cooed, as we made it peacefully to the 'you can now undo your seatbelt' phase of the journey.

It was only a 35 minute flight, but I painfully recollect now how each minute had passed by so slowly. I was on tenterhooks, at the ready to entertain you with the next trick the moment your concentration wandered. The passenger in the aisle seat even commended me on how well you had behaved, causing me to puff up with pride, but keeping on duty nonetheless. Thankfully we arrived without any incident at the busy little island airport where nan and grandpa met us with welcome hugs and kisses.

I remember, mummy, when I was a baby, my son shouts excitedly, bringing me back from my travels to the room. He places our photo on the book shelf and starts drawing a plane.

Being a Babe
the Devil Jumped Over

Sarah Thewlis

Castrillo de Murcia, Spain

If you ask me, a good deal of the participants in this year's baby-jumping ceremony leave a lot to be desired. When I'm in charge, I'll instate a minimum standard set of qualifications for being babes the devil jumps over. We'll have none of these teary-eyed pap-pukers. You know; the ones who dilute the solemnity of every fiesta with their dribbling. When I'm old enough to join the Holy Minervan Arch-Guild, and have a go at organising the Corpus Christi myself, we'll use only the sturdiest infants Castrillo de Murcia has to offer.

Just looking at all the fear and crying among my infant peers lately, you'd think no one had ever told them what an honour it is to be one of us; a new-born in Castrillo de Murcia, on the day the yellow-masked demon, Colacho, comes a-pouncing. Why there hasn't been a morning of the Corpus so far that one of them hasn't got spooked by how, raven-like in black, the Arch-Guild process through town with each hour the bells toll. And while I'm perfectly capable of sitting with Mamá through the daily church services, listening in awe to Colacho and the Drummerman percussing over our hymns in a ritual of sacred irreverence, inevitably one of the amateur squealers will chime in, giving a bad name to us all. I'll tolerate nothing of the sort when I get my turn at being Drummerman. I'll expel any dissenters from Mass with a swift tap of my drumstick to their bottoms!

My name is José Manuel de los Santos Pérez-Castidad and, in all my six months on this earth, I have been taught hourly to honour and respect the traditions of this town. Unlike some of these bottle-fed brats, I know the true value of being an infant obstacle in the Colacho's yearly corrida. I know what it means to my family, to my ancestors, to my pueblo, not to mention that pesky parasite of original sin who'll be quivering in my soul right now at the thought of being driven out by the devil's leaping. I know what it means for my future too. Anyone who ever grew up to be respectable in Castrillo de Murcia was lain down on the mattress in the street once, and witnessed the whoosh of a man's shoes overleaping his infant body. I intend to be the most respectable ex-baby ever to join the Holy Minervan Arch-Guild, and whatever else awaits me beyond that; the priesthood, the agricultural board, most certainly the Mayorhood. Having the devil jump over me, under the adoring eyes of all the townspeople, is just the first step in what is bound to be the most eminent career Castrillo de Murcia has ever seen. Just as my father and his father and his father before him began their illustrious careers with their performances under Colacho's feet, so I will enter the future annals of town history with the great work I do today.

Mamá mutters these things to me as she dresses me up in my finest linen playsuit. My father and brothers are in church already, doing their part as dutiful members of the Arch-Guild. Up until today it was my duty to go with them, and sit looking on jealously as Papa and Jaime lined up in the corridor of men bordering the altar, dressed in the sombre pitch of Guild-Butlers, their manly bodies topped by the plateaus of broad black hats. So far in the fiesta, I have served no function but to churn the melting-pot of envy and pride that bubbled up from seeing our second-born, Pepe, waiting at the back of the church in canary-yellow and felt. This year he is the Colacho's adolescent apprentice, a celebrated supporting role that has allowed him to spend the festival firmly in the centre of the towns-people's attention, dishing out beatings, both of the percus-sive and playfully violent kind.

Today I am not in church and today I am not jealous. On this morning of the eighth day of the Corpus, I am the biggest attraction, second only to Colacho himself, even if I will have to share my cushy stage with a band of lesser infants. Mamá ties me into my best bonnet. A slight breeze tends to come to our streets from far-off seaport towns and we don't want it to snake its way under the small collection of hairs I've been amassing on my head. With a yell to Abuela that shakes the farmhouse, Mamá takes me down-stairs and out onto the road. Abuela comes soon afterwards, jabbing her walking stick into the mud-track ahead as if it were the forceful pick of a rock-climber, burying itself in cliff-face. Our house is on the outskirts, to make room for all the land we own, but now we walk into the town centre in the sun and rumbling atmosphere of ceremony.

The cushions that will enthrone me have already been laid out near where crowds of parents and spectators are gathering. Beginning in front of the entrance to the church, a line of quilted pallets bisects the town square before worming down through the narrow alleyways where the more stage-fearing babies are watched by humbler crowds. Already my aunts and uncles have colonised the centremost mattress in the plaza with a cluster of tiny Pérez-Castidad cousins. I join them and wriggle into place next to cousin José Luis, who has been squeezed into a miniature dinner-jacket and smells of my tío Vicente's cologne. Abuela looks down at us, her wrinkles creasing into a smile as she calls us her men. The new-born of our cousin Virginia begins to wail on the pillow in front of us and I think of the inch of umbilical cord her shiny round tummy has yet to shed. That kind of behaviour is just about permissible in such a little one, but there really is no excuse for the rest of these hooligans with their bitten-down dummies and shop-bought booties. A lot of parents decide to stay by their darlings' make-shift bedsides to soothe the shameful caterwauling. Most of them won't even make a move when the Colacho comes, but will hover instead, ready to function as fleshy airbags in the nigh-on impossible event that the devil should fall. My Mamá knows me better than to insult me with such a safety net, and moves back with Abuela to their rightful place in the crowd. Only fearful Virginia stays, a tenter-hooked hoverer, besmirching our brave outpost with her motherly concern. I worry what God and the audience will think of this babyish spectacle of spittle and screams, but

64

thankfully the din in the church drowns us out as it reaches a parallel crescendo.

The priest emerges, shaded by a tan, velvet canopy that the canopy-carriers hold up on sticks. The Arch-Guild move out too, with my father and Jaime among them. The whole company files down towards us ceremonial lambs; an imposing procession of guild-members, flag-bearers and clergymen. Children are dressed in the glaring white of the brides of Christ whilst rows of green and yellow sashes tense against heaving chests of teenagers who've been press-ganged into dancing shufflingly for us. A whole constellation of the carnivalesque troops into my eye-line, driven on by the Drummerman's tattoo. No longer a focal point of the fiesta, young Pepe's apprentice mask is just a finger-painted splodge in the colourful crowd that hails the coming of his master.

The glorious retinue parts and I see Colacho at the foot of the mattress-chain before me. He is fearsome, even though I know he is only somebody's brother dressed up; even though I know he can only do me good by taking my sin with him as he passes. Through the corridor of human bodies, he radiates a weighty sense of awe. Because I am small, my eyes can't comprehend him in his tremendous entirety, but must rather scale his every terrible inch. His misleadingly mundane Nike trainers give way to blood-red fringes below the yellow that clothes the legs he will leap with. Loose at his calves and tighter round his thighs, it is the fabric my sin will cling to, the Velcro that will rip out the fuzz of evil inside me. I follow the red stripe on his yellow slacks up until I come to the cartoon flames and spikes of green hanging around his midriff, cut out in felt but still sharp to the sight. A ladder of crimson fabric spreads out across the front of his lemony fleece like an outline of his ribcage gone wrong. Although here and everywhere he bears the colours of our flag, Spain's vibrant 'Rojigualda', still he seems foreign and frightening. Nowhere is this foreignness more evident than his masked face, framed by the fleece's tasselled hood. I have seen the face before, of course, making appearances in every event the festival has to offer. It is different now that he is preparing to jump. The devil in him is real and close and sinister. Yellow as those cheery Simpsons, he is too dreadful to ever be TV-friendly. He has a single, black gash standing in for his eyebrows, atop holes through which human irises flash, circled by the mask's incongruously feminine eyelashes. Whoever painted his mouth seems to have gone for the look of a giant black bean, blotted onto the papier-mâché in a wobbly scream. His nose is too long, his face is too big, as if God had taken the pate of a goblin and stretched it out over the skull of a horse. All the blood in his head has pooled to two perfect red-circles on his cheeks. They mock me, along with the crude eyelash lines, by peppering this thing that frightens me with signs of femininity I know to be signs of weakness! I will not be mocked. I am not afraid. I'm an illustrious man of Castrillo de Murcia and I'm ready to receive the blessing I am owed.

Colacho begins the run-up to the first in the great line of leaps ahead of him. He is about to jump. The square is tense with the silence of anticipation and Colacho is paces away from leaping when a piercingly nasal, alien voice cuts through all ceremony and suspense. It shouts something in a language I don't understand, then seems to repeat this same thing in the language I do:

'Oh wait, please wait a second!' Through the ranks of familiar onlookers the alien bustles. Pale-skinned and female, she has hair the same colour as Colacho's sunny suit, with bright, blue eyes and made-up lashes to rival the mask's. My irritation at my fellow jumpees pales in comparison to the powerless indignation I feel at this new disruption. I have tended to look down on some of the lesser people of Castrillo de Murcia for their lapses in decorum, but this gilet-swaddled, selfie-stick-brandishing monstrosity makes me thankful for even my family's lowliest labourer's manners. She explains in the flustered tones of an apology that she has come all the way from Amsterdam, that her husband was from here and had wanted his baby to be overleaped. So appalled am I at the mention of impostor offspring that I barely even have time to be disdainful of the grating lisps and errors in her accent.

To my horror, this woman is greeted with nothing but murmurs of understanding from the townspeople and before I know it a baby is produced from the inelegant cats-cradle of plastic buckles and nylon she has strapped to her back. Again, I have barely a moment to sneer at the total lack of self-respect of any tot who allows himself to be lugged about in such a thing. She plops the pale gremlin down next to me on my mattress and my outrage begins to sizzle up to an intolerable breaking point. If you ask me, its hair is the colour of wee and it smells like sour milk and its clothes look like they're made of the stuff nappies are made of. It occurs to me that, much as I disapprove of the parents who feel the need to hover, at least it is their street to hover in, unlike this tourist who now ducks by her daughter's hand, grinning with giddy anticipation. It is so preposterous

I can't even understand how it has been allowed. I inherited my presence here from my father and his father and his father before him. I have spent my entire life preparing and rehearsing for, and deserving this moment. What has this thing, the daughter of a deserter of our town at most, done to earn her place on my mattress, in my streets, in my spotlight, in my traditions?

Colacho has begun his run-up again but I have been too full of anger to pay much attention. The old feelings of terror return at the sight of him, but this time around I have no clear headspace in which to steady myself. Before I know it he is a whole mattress closer to me and advancing steadily down the line in a saffron blur. Whenever Abuela makes me my potage it bubbles up in the pan all yellow and red, until she stirs it into a blurry orange. The speeding colours of Colacho blur too. My head does nothing but blend and bubble, adulterating my anger with fear. It all goes wrong.

My brain decides it will be panicked and confused instead of courageous.

I do what I always do when I'm cross; I hold my breath until my face goes blue. The devil doesn't jump over me. For the first time in her life, Mamá is forced to join the ranks of the hoverers, as she whisks my limpening body away. She takes me home and calms me down. Soon I am tired and decide to have a nap on my real mattress where it is quiet. The fiesta concludes without us.

You might have thought I'd mind not being a babe the devil jumps over, but it turns out, in avoiding it, I've had a greater evil overleap me. If they'd told me before this all started that our once-sacred tradition is now open to every suncreamed tourist who can afford his taxi here, well, I'd have had nothing to do with it. Maybe when my father and his father and his father before that took part it really meant something to be a babe the devil jumps over. But from where I'm crawling, it looks like I'll have a far better chance at being illustrious in this town if I'm the one ex-baby who refused to share his inheritance with strangers and held onto his own sliver of home-grown sin.

Remember Our DJ?

Cecile Sophie Bec

UK

Do you remember that time we spent in the back seat of the Punto? You, me, Baby Phil in the middle? Do you remember the car seat with the metal bars either side of it that stuck into our teenage girl fat hips? Our feet were up by our ears which didn't help, stretched above the lifetime supply of sleeping bags, holdalls and multi packs of Smartprice crisps. Poppy the hamster rattled her wheel and flicked sawdust at us all from her post on the back shelf. Possibly she wondered why she had been uprooted and placed in a stuffy tiny car full of angry loud teenagers and a baby boy. Or possibly she was comfortably oblivious. More so than you and I.

Long car journeys mean crumbs down your pants and in your cleavage. God, that did nothing to help my badly fitting bra become a more comfortable and useful appliance for my body. How was yours? I used to feel sorry for Phil too. He didn't look too breezy with all those sweaty crisp crumbs getting caught up in his nappy and seat straps. That particular long car journey also meant Baby

Phil as resident DJ. He sat well strapped into his small plastic throne, clutching onto the Tommee Tippee cassette player and mike, with Goosey Duck and Smokey Dog, his fluffy henchmen sitting either side of him, nodding in approval.

I don't know about you, but my favourite track of Baby DJ Phil's was 'This little bird flaps his wings, flaps his wings, flaps his wings, this little bird flaps his wings, flying away in the morning'. Haha! Oh come on, it was definitely the funkiest tune in the car! Solemn and Beaty. Almost like a pop song we wouldn't have been allowed to listen to. 'None of that Knives and Forks rubbish'. Mum's reasoning used to drive me up the wall! Still does really.

Do you remember you were always sleeping? Leaning on Phil's mini throne, probably trying to snooze away that silly summer?

'Stop leaning on the seat! I've got NO ROOM!' I shrieked. Hooray! Argument number 24 commences for the day!

'GET OFF. . . BRAT!' You yelled as you shoved the plastic baby box into me, squashing me against the door. Such a cruel big sister.

'YOU get off! Stop taking up ALL the room. . .! PRATT!' The worst insult of the family. Especially when bellowed with all your might from the very depths of your insides. 'Sebastian? Sir Prattsian more like!' Teehee, still proud of that one. Ultimate insult to the big brother.

Poor Old Phil was shaken about, left to right, right to left, head banging to Five Fat Sausages. I pushed with all my might against that plastic, defending the half square foot of room that'd been mine for the past five weeks. As If I was going to relinquish my space! The rage was mounting! Do

72

you remember how frizzy your hair would get from the damp warmth of the car? I don't think you were managing the Lizzy Bennet look too well, without the demure surroundings. I was attempting the Skater Girl look, but with a distinct lack of eyeliner and huge baggy jeans, I wasn't doing too well either.

'You Two Girls! Shut Up! Stop being so ridiculous or you can get out and walk!!'

I reckon at this point you probably shouted something about how you would rather be a gypsy than stuck in here with us complete twats. We could probably all die too. Goosey Duck's broken neck sagged and he stared, hating you and I for ruining his pride and challenging him to keep his floppy head upright. Baby Phil scooped him up and calmly reseated him in his position of power, then screamed;

'Where is Pots and Pans!!! I want Pots and Pans!!!'

Oh dear! The dreaded Pots and Pans! To be perfectly honest, I don't remember much about it apart from the fact that you hated it so much you ripped it out of the cassette player and threw it across the M1. Poor Baby DJ. Losing his prize compilation.

We can only be grateful for our baby brother that summer though. He saved us from what would have been a never-ending car journey of teenage anger and aggravated mother. OK, OK it was anyway. But there was a good healthy dose of innocent baby keeping us all a bit more sane, along with a few cheerful tunes. And you can't deny he had a cute face. I used to feel just a little bit cooler walking into a service station with Phil on my hip than I did without him.

Don't think I've forgotten the darker moments though. I know you haven't. You can't have done, no matter how good you were at pretending you weren't with us.

Little DJ was cheery enough in the day. But when he slept, he dreamed. And when he dreamed, he screamed. I suppose it isn't fun to bring it up again. But towards the end of those long weeks, do you think Mum even knew why she was driving any more? Did she know where she was taking us and what she was doing? The Travelodge we stopped at was full that night, or too expensive. Who knows, mum was probably just pacifying us for a moments peace. We drove and drove and it was cold and dark and Phil was starting to stir. I can picture you so well, even now. We'd stopped, somewhere on a bypass I think. Or it could have been a farm lay-by. Whatever it was, that big flash-light was right on Phil's face and he was getting angsty. You tried to shield his eyes with a book, but he was already gone. We were all angsty then.

'Why are we here?'

'We need to drive!'

'Phil will stop crying if we drive!'

'Mum!'

'I can't drive, I'll crash the car!'

'What is this creepy place?'

'Let's go to Auntie Catherine's.'

'Stop crying. . . look, Smokey Dog says stop.'

'Mum.'

'MUM!'

'I'll crash the car!'

'eeeaaaaAAAEHH!!'

Oh God.

And then, it ended.

'This is so. Stupid. It's our house too. We're all going home.'

I can still hear the exhaustion in her voice. She drove. Baby DJ Phil was quiet.

The Puffin, the Haunting and the Turtle

Sandy Bennett-Haber

Inner Hebrides, Scotland.

Taking our first sips of beer, we looked across to the diminutive island of Iona from the front facing beer garden of The Keel Row. We had earned these beers; having driven from Edinburgh, overnighted in Oban, taken the car on the ferry across to the Isle of Mull, and driven the slow island roads from Craigmure to Fionnphort. Whether it was our over cautious approach to the etiquette of the one lane roads, or our very occasionally pausing to take photographs, the proported one hour drive took us about three. All the while the lichen on the rocks glowed orange, the low grey clouds followed us and the steely water mimicked the sky. Ah Scotland – forever atmospheric. But on arrival the grey clouds had broken up and turned alto-cumulus; the evening sun transforming the waterfront vista to postcard perfection. We turned our Australian faces to the northern sun, sipped our beers and breathed the salty holiday air. Then the baby complained.

Having snoozed the day away under the hypnotic hum of a moving vehicle Rafa was ready for some crawling-exploring. Unfortunately the front yard of Fionnphort's pub doubles as grazing space for local sheep. This is not baby friendly. The sheep were not in residence, but their leavings were everywhere. We tried to distract Rafa by giving him a colourful bendy straw to chew: fail. His curious little self was determined to find sheep droppings every-time he was released from our arms, and determined to complain of mistreatment every-time he was restrained. Still for half an hour or so summer in Scotland was glorious. It was well worth the journey, and the juggling of a wriggly resentful baby on your knee to drink our half pints in the Hebridean sunshine.

The 'we' I speak of is myself, new mum; my mum, doting first time nanna over on a visit from Australia and my ten month old son Raphael– English dad, Aussie mum, born in Scotland. With my husband away with work elsewhere in Scotland, and me still on maternity leave it seemed the perfect time do the tourist thing. We would get out of the city, see some new parts of Scotland, and have someone else do the cooking and bed making for a few days, ie relax. Perfect plan!

We (being my husband and I) had already driven Rafa from Scotland to England, flown him to Vietnam, then Australia, New Zealand and America, followed by a short three week road trip to Canada and back into the States, before returning to England and driving back to Scotland; a little midweek jaunt up to the islands seemed childsplay after our four months living out of suitcases. True, since our return to 'normal' life I had loved getting into something of an evening routine with the baby, but what is life if you don't shake up your routine now and again.

Summertime in Edinburgh means long summer evenings, it is not overly warm, but it is light until 10pm. This is lovely – unless you are trying to get your baby to sleep at 6pm, and despite your best efforts at double layered curtains and blackout blinds it is still very very light in your baby's room. Summertime farther north in Scotland it is light until at least 11pm and nowhere we stayed seemed to take this into even the slightest consideration with their curtaining solutions. Some days I question whether it is really necessary to have a dark room to get Rafa to sleep at night. These are the days when he goes to sleep quickly and easily. Every time I have difficulty getting him to sleep the light streaming into the room is one of my earliest culprits.

The baby *usually* sleeps well, but occasionally on our overseas trip we encountered what we called 'the haunted house' phenomenon – where for no apparent reason our normally placid, deep sleeping fellow screams the house down, refuses to respond to any of our calming techniques and eventually passes out in a trembling, hiccuping mess. Leaving us having sung ourselves hoarse, with our nerves torn to shreds, staring at each other wide eyed and – if we are still talking to each other at that point, we reassure ourselves that he does not do this very often, and that there must be something about the place that sets him off.

With its history of long bitter winters, lonely shepherds, lonelier wives, home made drink, misadventure and lost treasure, we should have known that a haunted night was likely on the Isle of Mull. Then again the rough night we experienced could have been due to yanking Rafa out of his routine, bunking him in a car for two days and then rewarding our sociable cherub by strapping him into a high chair, giving him a lot of attention from pretty waitresses, tasty treats to chew through with his four teeth, and then trying to get him to sleep in a room with thin curtains. It seemed like a good idea at the time.

At eight pm we wondered if perhaps he had gotten a little over stimulated, at nine pm we wondered if it was his teeth that were bothering him, at ten pm we gave up trying to get him to sleep and had him watch a DVD with us, and at eleven pm with a red faced screaming and exhausted child everything seemed like a bad idea, and we were wondering if our B&B hosts would be allowing us to stay the second night, and did we really want to stay in a what was clearly a badly curtained, haunted house anyway?

He did eventually go off to sleep, and nerves shattered so did we. My mother and I slept late and when we shamefacedly went into breakfast our host happily jostled a smiling Rafa on her knee while we ate. Both were oblivious to there ever having been the slightest hiccup in the bed time routine.

The puffin pilgrimage was a pre-baby dream. I had wanted to see the cartoon cute birds since my early days in Scotland. Somehow though the summers always filled with other things, and then I was pregnant and couldn't go on a puffin boat, and then I had a new baby and couldn't go on a puffin boat. Part of our Hebrides plan was that I would get to see puffins. That morning it was raining, I was running late and feeling like a shattered slummy mummy. I could barely remember how to brush my own teeth, let alone why I wanted to see puffins. But, nevertheless I was booked on a boat trip out to Staffa and my mum was all set to Rafa wrangle until my midday return. The only thing between me and the puffins was me and my inability to put one foot in front of the other.

Somehow even with my slug brain and the slow island roads we made it just in time. I waved a hasty goodbye, clambered on-board and breathed. This morning out was a rare treat – it promised puffins, wilderness *and* me time. Then, just when all the hurdles seemed surmounted, island time slipped in, and we stopped to wait for late tourists.

The six mile boat journey from the Isle of Mull to Staffa takes around thirty five minutes, but I had been in the boat for more than that already, and not gotten any closer to the puffins. My carefully pre-arranged post trip meeting time was adrift. My text messages were not sending. I tried to relax into the enforced stillness, but my smidgen of travel zen spluttered out.

At last we were off, the rain was clearing, the water was calm, the sacred isle, Iona, with her medieval religious houses, was stone skippingly close, but the phone signal was no better. Off the west coast of Scotland, on a glassy Hebridean sea, all I felt was frustration. I was failing at one of the most fundamental challenges of travel: to be in the moment. I didn't want to be in this moment. I was yearning to be back and we had hardly begun. I wasn't in touch with the ancient Celtic goddess within. I was in touch with the stressed out, time poor mum I already knew, and I didn't need to travel to the Inner Hebrides to meet her.

And then a fin and a tail surfaced. The dolphins were out to play. Swimming alongside the boat, jumping, frolicking merrily in front of us, flirting with the myriad cameras. I oooh'd and aaah'd with everyone else. I was fleetingly in the moment.

Approaching Staffa, I tried to hold onto my dolphin calm, but the impatient lady crept back. Yes, Celts, Vikings, shepherds, musicians, and botanists found the geological columnar splendour splendid, and perhaps the island was the only remnant of the Giant's Causeway in Scotland, but mystical properties, basalt columns, hexagonal rock formations, volcanic eruptions, and musical caves aside, I needed to know if I going to see puffins? And maybe Fingal's Cave? And what time were we going to get back to Fionnphort? And how was I going to let mum know I was delayed? And was the baby ok?

I strode over the lush grassy terrain of the island. More alert to being slowed down by the lady with inappropriate footwear ahead of me, than the picturesqueness or otherwise of the island – sturdy with good tread she wore not. In my well worn walking boots I overtook her on a particularly uneven, muddy patch. I was headed – at long last – to the designated puffin watching spot, and nothing was going to get in my way.

I am no twitcher, but I do know that patience is a required virtue of the feathered wildlife pilgrim, I just didn't know if I still had it post baby. At the far end of the island I shuffled about, pondering the merits of each vantage point. There were gulls above and shags in the rockpools below, but not a cartoon cute puffin to be seen. Finally, at the edge of the grassy cleft, looking back towards the jetty I chose my spot, and waited on the salt blown precipice.

And there it was – my heart stopped – a silver flash of fish, clamped in an orange beak appeared, and then vanished into the ferns. I saw it – *I saw it.* Was there a burrow in the crags just below where I was staked out? I crept cautiously closer to the edge. Was there a puffling right at this moment feasting on fish brought in by mum or dad? Was that happy puffin warbling I could hear? I waited with my head cleared of phone checking, clock ticking and baby fretting. I had seen a puffin going into the front door of its summer house! True it was just for a moment – but I could very well see another, in the rocks below, or on the opposite cliff or. . . *right in front of me!*

Yes, there it was, in the grassy fern, right by me: a wee puffin. Smaller than I had imagined, sleek white belly, black skull cap, white face, orange beak – looking out to sea, holding its pose in profile. I was standing quietly in the puffins' wilderness and there was one close enough to be put in my pocket. My phone – no good for anything else, took quite a good picture of my new little friend.

The quiet puffin watchers on the other side of the cliff spotted it, but the prize was mine. I had journeyed all this way and a puffin had come to visit me.

On the way back I was once more attached to my mobile phone. A couple of messages from my bewildered mother had come through, but I couldn't reassure her that I had not been kidnapped by Vikings and was only waylaid by island time. This was her holiday as well and I was guilt ridden that she was stuck waiting rather than able to go off and do exploring of her own. And guilty as well for having gone off gallivanting by myself. Yes last night I would have gladly traded Rafa in for a puffin – but today was a new day and I missed him.

Back on dry land at last a fretful mummy was reunited with her relaxed baby and her only slightly concerned mother. With the sun out we headed towards the nearby crescent of beach. There was no particular path marking out how to get down to the sand, but this was no obstacle to we three generations of beach loving folks. We gamely carried Rafa's pram the short distance down clumps of grassy dunes and plonked ourselves on the sand. Apart from a few dog walkers ambling by we had the place to ourselves. The tide was out and the sun shone on the remaining rivulets.

While I hastily gulped down a salad roll Rafa got gritty sand under his pudgy knees and delightedly inspected the flotsam and jetsam of the island beach: cray baskets, seaweed, shells, driftwood, bottle tops and small sea creatures. After the baby trauma of the previous night, and the hectic flavour of the morning, this was the holiday as it should be. Rambling on an empty beach, letting the baby roam about of his own accord. Keeping close, but letting him follow his own instincts; his attention span for each new thing was short, and the classic baby exploration technique of putting everything into his mouth was well utilised. And then he discovered the water.

My mother tells me that as a youngster growing up on the south eastern coast of Australia I would frequently put my head down and crawl into the waves. Rafa, following his mother's mer-person habits eventually eschewed the semi-dry beach and crawled into the unexpectedly warm water – not quite warm enough to tempt the adults beyond their ankles, but plenty warm enough for Rafa. The low tide provided a good run of shallow water, and we managed to get most of Rafa's clothes off before he became weighed down by wet wool.

We had seen time and time again on our travels in Australia, New Zealand and America that his happiness elevated whenever he was in the water. A happy chap anyway, he became nothing short of 'bliss-ed out' in the water. Rafa has been dunked, or has dunked himself into the water all around the world. He is at his happiest when river currents are washing around him and waves are buffeting him. One of my sadnesses at the end of our family trip had been knowing he would not have as many outdoor swimming opportunities in Scotland. Yet, here he was now, in Scotland, determinidly moving his little body through the shallows, resembling nothing so much as a sea turtle about to ride the currents over to Iona.

Not finding it quite warm enough to follow suit, we packed ourselves up quick smart, jumped on the next ferry and picked him up on the other side. (Or we let him paddle about until he started looking a little blue and then dried him off, scraped as much sand as we could out of his fat folds, dressed him in a nice dry outfit and all took the ferry together. . .) Either way I can categorically state that Iona is not haunted. Rafa slept while we dawdled through the remains of the nunnery, drinking our coffees while basking in Scottish sunshine and imagining the cloistered lives of those who had lived within the walls. We walked about, taking in the cairns on hills we would not explore on this trip, salivating at the provender of organic gardens which we would not taste, and finally just sat on the white sands, watched the world go by and breathed the salty holiday air.

The break part of my mini-break was not after all the part without the baby, it was while he was playing at my feet and snoring quietly at my side, dreaming of life as a sea turtle.

The Mind of a Toddler

Marcia Ulrich

USA

On a stifling hot, humid summer day we set off on a drive to visit some of our old neighbors. Brian and Lisa had lived across the street from us for close to three years. During that time we became very good friends. They had a son, Brandon, who was the same age as my son, Christopher. It was wonderful to have a playmate for both Chris and his older sister, Beth. We were very sad when Brian was transferred and they moved four hours away. It had been a quite awhile since we had seen them, so we planned this long anticipated visit.

We loaded up the car, buckled the children in their car seats and set off on our trip. Did I mention that it was an extremely hot day? Well, it was. We had an older car that did not have air conditioning. Due to the extreme heat it was necessary to travel with all the windows down. It did not take long to begin to feel windblown, sticky and wishing the trip was at an end. Not to mention the roar of the wind necessitated almost yelling to be heard. Needless to say, there was very little conversation.

After about three hours on the road, I hear this little voice coming from the back seat, 'Mommy, mommy'. It took me a few minutes to realize that it was Christopher trying to get my attention. I turned around in my seat to look at him to make sure I could hear him well enough to attend to his needs. He looked at me with a quizzical expression and said, 'Mommy, how did God make the earth?' Where did that come from?? For a moment, I contemplated how to answer that trying to yell above the roar. It only took me that moment to reply, that we would talk about it later.

Obviously, the heat and roar of the road did not interfere with my toddler's thought process.

An explanatory note on the inclusion of *Eva's Unexpected Journey*

Initially, on reading Gary Yelen's retelling of his mother's memories of her escape from Nazi Germany, I set the story aside as not fitting with the theme of the book. Eva was in Gary's words 'definitely not a baby, just a young confused child.' However, putting the finishing touches on this collection amid the Syrian refugee crisis made it abundantly clear to me that something was missing.

Travel is for many synonomous with holiday, exploration, relaxation and escape from everyday life. For some that escape is a one way ticket. Single people, couples, grandparents, mothers, fathers, children and babies can all find themselves hurled into the wild unknown because conflict has torn the hinges off their doors. The inclusion of *Eva's Unexpected Journey* seeks to make a small acknowledgment of the many, many familes from war torn countries for whom travel is an unexpected rupture from the known into an uncertain future.

Eva's Unexpected Journey

Gary Yelen

Germany

The night was one of ominous comings. The hum of thunder was in the distance, the lights would soon flicker, candles were taken from the drawers and laid in their usual spots in preparation for the coming darkness. It rained heavier and seemed impossibly darker that night and the house lay awake for the air was thick with foreboding. If we dared to close our eyes or move we were sure to suffocate.

The morning proved otherwise. Hannah met me at the gate as usual, the clouds were slowly parting and light was bringing the glorious jewelled droplets to life, trees and shrubs alike dripped their precious lodgers upon us, spiders' webs glistened with tiaras and speckled necklaces; the yellow stars newly pinned to our tunics, by our mothers, made us feel we belonged to the morning and the place. We began to dance and skip a little and school seemed a pleasant destination to share our joy.

The severe lines of her jacket and skirt seemed more stiff than usual on the headmistress this morning. Unusually she stood at the front gate, quite erect, still and sombre. Almost imperceptibly, she stiffened further as Hannah and I approached. Her hands reached out clasping ours. She bent down, almost on bended knee, drawing us even closer.

'Go home now Eva, Hannah, go and do not return.' She whispered quietly.

'But why?' I whispered back, unconsciously mimicking her tone.

'Go now, your parents will explain.' Bewildered, tears beginning to flow freely, I grabbed Hannah's hand and we ran, the morning no longer holding any joy, the night seemingly upon us again.

We got home, having barely breathed in our escape from whatever pursued us; we ran from what we did not know, a look, a word, a smell of some unknown beast. Hannah released my hand and ran straight home. I crashed through our front door tumbling over several suitcases already laid out in the hallway. Mother came rushing from the kitchen cheeks as stained as mine. She grabbed me as I flew into her arms and we held each other until we had sqeezed the last tears from our exhausted bodies.

'Eva, we are going on a long journey,' mother begun, 'your father will be home shortly, he and Hannah's father are buying tickets for a bus and boat trip, and we must be ready to leave on his return. We may not be coming back so go upstairs now and fill your pockets with the things that are precious to you. I have already packed your bag, so we are ready.'

'Why mama?' I asked confused and bewildered by the happenings of the morning.

'The world has gone mad, and we must go, and go quickly before the madness overtakes us.'

The sense of urgency was not lost on me as I ran upstairs to fill my pockets. I had no idea with what. My most precious possession was a little quartz pebble Hannah had found in the park and handed to me, accompanied by a little kiss on the cheek. Nothing else seemed that important at that moment, so I put the pebble in my jacket pocket and went downstairs to wait by the door for father's return.

We were squashed up the back as the bus rolled slowly through the darkened streets. The only sounds were the occasional groan of the bus as it navigated the corners of our blacked out town and the accumulated whispers of those huddles together in front of us. As we reached the outskirts the road straightened and the bus quickened.

Although I thought I knew most people aboard it was hard to tell who was who as hats were drawn down low and coat collars upturned. Most deceiving themselves that shrouds would hide them from the unknown evil permeating the murky light. Mist filled moonbeams encroached on our hidden faces.

The bus headed towards the coast, the peculiar urgency of the occasion frustrated by the meandering route the driver had chosen to take.

Hannah and I once again held hands tightly. Our bond for life was forged ever stronger through each torturous minute and second. Our parents were not part of the hum of whispers, but sat silently, steely faces ashen, time taking its toll, ticking their breath away.

The lights of the port could be seen in the distance now, our parents finally joined the whispers of the bus, which in no time turned into an excited, expectant almost giggling party atmosphere. The driver explained over the loud-speaker that we would have to depart quickly, but we were to stay orderly. Those with surnames from A to J would go to left and those from K to Z would go right. The boats that waited at port were already billowing smoke. Their cargo, human animals – caged by a fear that had swept the country – were about to be transported away from all they knew.

The bus was directed to pull in close to a large shed. We rose slowly, father making sure we had all our luggage. I was still clutching tightly to Hannah's hand as we made our way to the front, my parents ahead of us, Hannah's behind.

As we exited the bus two men diverted us into our alloted alphabetical queues. It hadn't dawned on me until this point that Hannah's and my surnames were at different ends of the alphabet. Before I had time to plead we stay together her parents had shuffled her off to their allotted queue. I screamed to Hannah to come back, but she was lost in the urgency of survival and was heading towards the boat behind ours.

Families, packed together, moved in a quick shuffle. Parents clung tightly to their children and luggage, moving towards the long wooden ramps that would lead us to our unknown futures. Our family was one of the last to board, and quite quickly the seamen and wharfies dislodged grand ropes and great rumbling engines vibrated through the ship. With great turbulence of waters the vessel moved slowly away from its lodgings.

A small cheer, maybe it was a cumulative sigh, emanated from those aboard. For a moment I was caught up in the hesitant euphoria but then I demanded my parents let me see if Hannah's ship was following. They allowed me to go look from the rear of the ship as long as I returned quickly. I pushed and shoved my way through to the back and could just make out Hannah's ship pulling away from the port's edge through the thickening fog.

I went back to join my parents and reported that the ship had just moved away from the port. Only then did I think to ask my mother where we were going and how long it would take. I was eager to be reunited with Hannah and explore our imaginings of our future lives.

As mother was beginning to explain how our travels could possibly unfold a murmur began to emanate from the rear of the ship, then howls and increasing screams. What could have happened? I forced my way back, my throat tightening as I pushed and forced my way to the rear railing. I was struggling for breath, I couldn't speak there was nothing to say, I just stood, stared into the distance as tears soaked my face. I could see the gun boats forcing Hannah's ship back to port.

I never saw Hannah again. The quartz crystal I had made into a necklace and to this day it remains close to my heart.

In Passing Years

David Wilkie

The day had been longer,
Now stronger in her own
Resolute way, she stepped on

Gone her tears, yet
passed unconsciously
To myself...

As she carried me
Desperately seeking
Somewhere
Just anywhere,
Anyone...
That she could pass me to

Years would follow
Of that day
The last journey I had
With my mother...

I recall so well
telling as I do now.

As I, in my own way,
oh for that day,
Never to have been.
And yet, yet
I carried my own children
but as a father,
Rather than let go
Dear Lord, how I,
Yes I, held on to my own

Son, grand, his mother
My own blood. . .
Floods of tears, in passing
Years, our journey goes on
Forever more. . .

Bonny Dundee –
A Modern Family Fairy Tale

Jo Smith

Scotland

It was a grey day crossing the firth.

Angela tried to keep her spirits up under the low cloud and rain, and the strangeness of the circumstance. Fighting to silence the nagging query in the back of her mind, 'why venture all this way, to a city you barely know?' Yet, here she was, alone, on a cold January morning, bringing her new-born baby son to see a woman whom she had met only once.

The train trundled across its low bridge, and she gazed out over turbulent water, disconcerted by the proximity of the lapping waves below. Archives, sepia images of an historic bridge disaster flashed through her mind. She adjusted the carrier straps and pulled her baby in closer, hand gently cradling the soft pulse of his warm head. As she reached for the powder-blue bonnet which had arrived in the mail, carefully wrapped in tissue paper and ribbons, she was engulfed by vivid visions reeling past – bricks crumbling, carriages tumbling, a leap, a jump, a scream, frantically kicking her way up through icy water. Her heart raced. It was not exactly the fear of bridge collapse which startled her. It was the sudden recognition of a powerful, primordial instinct – the overwhelming protective love she felt towards this child.

At that moment, she knew that from now on, she would do anything to escape chaos and disaster for the sake of the small boy she carried. He had already turned her life so completely upside down, and now, the merest hint of a risk had her imagining the worst and working out how best to keep him safe. Since the baby was strapped to her chest in the '*Mother's favourite 'Babycare comfort carrier 500' with matching changing bag*', her underwater alter ego would have to lean back and kick, whilst holding the baby's head above the waves. Her heart rate gradually came back to rest as the contingency plan took shape in her mind. It would be okay. They would resurface immediately if the worst happened, and they would make it to the other side. A phrase, perhaps a prayer, came to the front of her mind; blood is thicker than water, blood is thicker than water.

The train drew nearer and started to lurch as it rounded the bend. The baby stirred but did not cry. Noisy passengers began to gather in the gangway, swinging heavy luggage bags down from shelves and slinging them onto their backs. She huddled as far into the window-side as possible to avoid any renegade blows. The baby made a series of scrunched up faces as a sudden cool draught blew across his tiny cheeks, rousing him from the last remnants of his sleep. Eyes widened and blinking, together, mother and child felt the rumble of the changing tracks through their bones as the train slipped off the bridge rails and onto standard tracks with a clunk and a grind. His 6-week-old brow furrowed deeply and his enquiring eyes tried to follow the sounds of the gangway crowd, up and to the left. The sound of well-meaning, patronising voices filled her head – one of those vacuous phrases people had said time and time again. 'There's nothing wrong with his hearing anyway!' Except that today there were no well-wishers around to say it. No health visitors, midwives, aunties, neighbours, friends.

'Just me,' she thought.

'Just the baby and me.'

'It's you and me kiddo,' she said out loud. 'We better get used to it!'

He looked at her but did not cry, and of that she was glad, not wishing for him to draw any attention their way. There was an odd sensation of delight that came from being anonymous, away from the clutches of all those ooh-ing and ah-ing well-wishers. At the same time, she was aware of just how vulnerable and alone they both were, heading into a city of strangers, with nothing but each other.

Planning how to manoeuvre herself off the train with the baby and the buggy and all their things was the next trick. Should she prepare now and stand with the others in the doorway? No, she decided, imagining a shunt into the bumpers at the station. She stayed seated until the last possible moment, and then attempted to un-collapse the buggy. It was supposed to be an 'easy-up; flexible shopper' but the myriad tricks and clips had caught her out already at the start of the journey, not least searching for the elusive catch for the brake, so that the buggy started moving away each time she went near! Slowly, they pulled to a stop, she got the thing unfolded and made her way onto the platform.

They'd been travelling for a few hours now. The baby would be hungry again soon, and she would have to find someplace to feed him in the city. She did not relish the thought of sitting in a grubby plastic cubicle in the railway station's public toilet. It had the kind of cleaner who, with her cigarette-breath, slop-of-the-mop-trailing-a-metal-bucket and faded blue overcoat, looked more like a harbinger of dirt and disease than a weapon in the fight against germs. Perhaps there would be a Boots or Mothercare in a shopping centre, or a small café? Looking at the surrounding buildings from here: a ship museum, a tiny airfield for light aircraft, towering university buildings; this idea didn't look promising, and indeed it took some time to find a suitable place. It was a greasy café. Not quite what she had in mind, but adequate.

She took out the streetmap and tried to identify her route to the address. What was she thinking? They couldn't even be sure of a warm reception! Certainly it had all been perfectly civil, that day, when he took her, unannounced, to meet his mother.

She felt like his shameful secret. Seventeen. Seven months pregnant.

His mother did well to hide any outward signs of the disillusionment she must have felt inside. That, at least, Angela reasoned, was considerate. But without him there, would she see a different side to this woman? Would now be the time for a tirade of her *real* feelings on the whole matter? Would she even want to know?

102

Pushing the buggy up the steep cobbled streets towards the crescent, she remained resolved. There was no way to be sure what was waiting, but she decided to simply trust and give it a shot.

As cheerily and confidently as she could muster, Angela talked to her baby boy in the sing-song 'motherese' voice that makes everything ok.

'Come on then, my handsome little man! Let's go up to Grandma's house, shall we?'

The baby gurgled and blew some bubbles on his tiny lips. They continued on their way, with hopeful steps. How could anyone not love him, least of all a grandmother? Blood is thicker than water after all.

Blue Sarong

Helen Sheil

East Gippsland, Australia

Who can say what is remembered
and what re-remembered
from the telling of stories
triggered by photographs
of early travels?

There is a picture of you
wrapped in my blue sarong
lying in the sand dunes.
I wonder what you remember
of times spent watching the grass
create patterns on fresh blown sand
or the sparkle of sunlight on the Marlo inlet.
Do you remember
the sounds of water lapping,
gulls calling or the feeling
of the warm ocean breeze on your skin?
Sentient qualities
that can be tracked like DNA?

We camped on our travels.
Some thought it
a challenging landscape for a child:
sticks, rocks, prickly plants and insects,
scrub under the tall gums
but you appeared happy
on these expeditions.

In the pictures there are always children
from other families
who also chose to live in the country.
At *Forests Forever* camps
child-care was in the river.
Do you remember finding coloured stones
to make paint and decorate our bodies?
There are pictures of you swinging on ropes
at Barbara and Etienne's place
into crystal clear water.

Campfires feature in the photos.
The hearth of our gatherings.
It was the place people shared stories.
You won't remember the conversations
of owner-builder disputes.
The battle between those
benefiting from extractive industries
and new settlers
committed to reclaiming land
ravaged by blackberries, rabbits,
clear felling and mining.
These disputes between

the 'red' and the 'green' turned nasty.
Other children's parents prosecuted
for living in illegal dwellings
spent time in prison, sequentially:
First the Dad's in Pentridge,
then on their release the mothers,
incarcerated in Fairlea women's prison.
One mother wrote from her cell
that was smaller, dirtier and colder
than the cosy 'illegal' dwelling she had built (1985).
But I suspect what you remember
is the food and friendliness
of this larger camping 'family'.

Backpacks feature in the photos.
I was grateful to campers
who took turns carrying you and Clancy
in backpacks and slings keeping you snug.
It was frosty camping at Waratah Flat,
the clearing circled by blood red flowering waratahs.
Did the constant drone of debates
between botanical experts
comparing seeds and leaf types of different tree species
and the best place to find native orchids
pass over you as background chatter
or did a sense of the beauty seep into your consciousness?

Then there are Mallacoota camping photos
that began when you were in a bassinet
and continued 'til you left home.
The Easter parade features constantly.

Do you remember
the rhythm of the gumboot boogie
conducted by a gifted Grunden?
Or later crafting giant birds,
exotic animals or sea creatures for the parade?
Did the themes and images of the
Carnivals in Coota merge over time?
The jester in '*Magic and Movement*'
or Da Vinci's figure in '*A question of balance*'?
Maybe the linked black and white hands of '*Kindred spirits*,'
the pelicans in '*Familiar shore*'
or the iconic Australian images of '*Animals and Artists*'
followed by those of countries
connected by the Southern Ocean: South America and Africa?

A favourite picture
is of you and Clancy and on Mt. Ellery
a place you first saw from Robbie's shoulders,
when he scaled the rocks like a spider
to share this breath taking beauty
with you, his daughter.

Every spring there were new places to explore.
Did this enchantment
inspire your return as an adult
to tackle the *Cloudwalk*,
a memorable experience
with hailstones on the tree ferns
and night arriving before the trip was half over.

Now when you camp in other countries
do you think of these camping rituals?

The fires to sit by?
The shared food?
Do you trek to memorable places
to watch the sun rise
and remember the koori dancers
welcoming in the new millennium
while Uncle Albert told creation stories
and dolphins swam in the waves?

When you watch the sun sink over new horizons
do you remember looking out over Gabo Island
or being serenaded onto Betka Beach at sunset
with saxophones playing?

I wonder what you remember
of making sand sculptures.
Is it the detail of the Snowy River
running from the mountains to the sea
or the rocking chair?
A simple chair with a rock on the seat

Maybe it's the sound of the ocean pounding nearby
and the skill of the hands and minds
that created these beautiful sculptures?

Since you left on your own travels
I eagerly read your stories.
Just like when you were little,
you still share your views of the world with me.
I've found answers to my unspoken questions
of what impact this lifestyle

of minimal home comforts but closeness
to natures nourishing terrain* had –
not only on you
but on the landscape to which you belong.
It seems mother earth also smiles on your travels
while welcoming you home when you return?

*Acknowledgement to Deborah Bird Rose for the term
'nourishing terrain' (1997)

Struck by Innocence

Stacey Campbell

Scotland- Australia

You won't remember this – nor will you remember me – but I can see your soft hand reaching out across the aisle to clutch the finger of a pleasant stranger sitting beside you. I can still see your gaze; a look of easefulness and mild curiosity as the passenger smiled at you while your head lay upon your mother's shoulder. The enormity of your chestnut eyes reminded me of warm nights spent with family, each of us in comfortable silence as we read or played or wrote. You were just a small creature, entirely innocent and oblivious to your bravery. A bold little thing as you reached out both to give and receive comfort. It was a simple gesture, and by all means an ordinary one, but as I sat with a book in my lap for the long flight back home I felt like I had glimpsed a reason why I wanted to return. Not merely to my home and family, but to the woman I had been before I thought I needed this journey.

It began with a broken heart. My own, to be precise. Months passed by in a daze of melancholy but in my head I measured by seasons. By Spring I was feeling that peculiar emotion of pining – you know, that feeling of achiness inside that tells you something is missing? I attempted to sate the cravings with poetry and meandering walks by the coast, but somehow the words lost their meaning and the warm Spring air sent more tears streaming from my eyes. By Summer, I did the unthinkable and cast brief words his way. The reply was as amicable and warm as it had always been but the words I'd so badly wished to share with him were gone; no longer would I respond to this heartache.

It was the kind of emptiness that altered the mind and tested the spirit; an absence which wracked the entire body with unwanted feeling. And it was right at the moment when I felt like the stitches holding my heart together were ready to be removed, healing complete and organ intact, that I discovered the truth. Nothing ever quite prepares you for the moment when you find out they've moved on. Or that she was in such close proximity to yourself that you could have known her. Or that the words you thought were affection turned out to be cowardly misgivings. Flashes of the tenderness you thought you knew dissipated into the air like black smoke from a snuffed fire. The seam holding my heart together came undone and, quite simply, I fell apart.

The healing process is not ever what others make it out to be. Happiness does not appear on a particularly bright sunny morning, or after finding money you'd forgotten about in your pocket. No, it's not like that at all. It's more of a slow and deliberate amnesia; a willingness to forget the memories and block them from resurfacing. But amidst this healing, there is an ocean of misery in which you find your-self – it takes your life and soul to kick your arms and legs enough to keep afloat. It's the tedious and seething pain of having to take a threaded needle to the seams of your broken heart in order for it to reflect its whole self again. It's the momentary joy that the bliss of ignorance brings you when you find yourself forgetting your own sadness. It's the moment when you are in pieces, held together by your own bravado that you appear strong and self-contained and even happy. You're a fool and you've even fooled yourself.

By Autumn I had taken to the bed of a stranger who would soon become more familiar to me than his memory. We lay as one: intertwined in lust but entangled in our own desire for intimacy. An encounter which required no commitment, only presence. I could gaze at him and press my head to his neck but he knew I meant no harm. He could hold my hand and stroke my back but he knew I would not embroider extra stitches in this lovers' blanket. We enshrouded each other in this veil of touch; proximity of skin with its softness enough to soothe rough edges. I blinked back the memories that threatened to encroach upon this scene. Instead I held my head up high as I straddled his thick body. I shook away self-doubt and insecurity. I lay with him as if I'd done this many times before. I acted brave and unbroken. When I came home, I let myself cry.

There was no doubt I was restless. Crippled by the fear of being alone yet yearning for solitude where I wouldn't have to hide my misery. Keeping still cast my mind into spells of the bleak unknown so, instead, I walked. I walked up and round the winding hills of the Scottish wild, down steep ridges where my knees knocked gritty rocks protruding from the grass. I grappled with pathways ribbed with tree roots that rose like ribcages from the ground. I journeyed past the vast country fields that by now the wind had whipped a shore of amber leaves upon. I knew where I was yet I felt disoriented, as if the people around me were moving with such rapidity and precision that all I could do was merely stand at the side in my own disbelief. I longed for adventure as if a foreign place would somehow provide the answer to whatever question my subconscious was posing.

'What's wrong?' they would ask me.

'I'm fine.' The lie was as natural as the grief. I suppressed my thoughts of him so desperately that I would often dream about what happened between us, waking up in the wee hours of the morning feeling unsettled and solemn, forgetting why I was unhappy and like I'd lost something. *What happened to me?* I would ask. *Where are you?*

I still measured by seasons. Winter arrived in Scotland like a whisper: a hush of frost concealing the black trees with an icy fur. It took me by surprise for when I looked outside the snowfall was silent and sombre as the glowing embers of Autumn faded out. I cried more than was probably necessary. I let the anger bubble within me like a dormant volcano before erupting with such irrevocable fury that when it was over, all I could do was look at the ashes I left myself with and the destruction I had caused. Baffled and overwhelmed by emotion, I hadn't yet destroyed myself. But if I stayed here any longer I would.

Shortly after I found myself in another hemisphere; a land of dreams and possibility where I thought the Gold Rush was a reference to the yellow sun splitting in the sky. The heat had hit me like my heartbreak – just as sudden and strange and harsh. I had come from a bitter Scottish winter where ice slicked the streets like black snakes and wind ripped through dense forest like a beast's roar. Now I feared the penetrating glare of the Australasian sun and the possibility of confronting creatures I'd only ever imagined before. My fears dispelled as I basked in time spent with family. Engaged in unexpected conversation and frank exchange of the things that mattered to me but which I'd forgotten. And even when I found myself alone, I was utterly content, watching this other world as I relished the warmth of the shadows and the mildness of the evening sun. The heat exhausted me and I would eventually fall asleep unthinkingly and for the entirety of the night. To be alone but feeling less than lonely was the beginning of something I had not felt in months.

Each morning I would awaken beneath the early light of the implacable sun, rising with a rush of enthusiasm for the day's possibility ahead. How alien it felt to examine the wilderness of a land so incredibly arid and dry: a heat stifling and penetrating; both a desert and an industrial maze. I explored vast caves and exotic animals; the peculiar ebb of the Indian Ocean which was so unlike the Atlantic. I spent hours in the evening, jotting down new thoughts furiously in my journal as the sun set in an amber haze – the kind of unique and unashamed perspective that only distance can bring. The power I had over my life – over my plans, my body, myself – was as incredulous as it was palpable. I felt wonder-filled; mostly amazed at how far I could take myself but, surprisingly, a little sad that I was yet to feel myself. But like this blazing sun before me, I knew I would rise again; as high and as bright and as one.

I am unsure why your gaze struck me so – it was a moment of unabashed affection which stirred a desire in me I hadn't yet known. I don't recall you crying the entire eight hour flight either. Perhaps the 40 degree heat of another hemisphere had exhausted you too. I wonder if you, like me, had found yourself on a beach with sand like white flour on Christmas day, another ocean as clear and azure as the endless sky, surrounded by family amidst the unfamiliarity of another country's climate and customs. I wonder if you were feeling as far away but as safe as I. I thought back to a couple of months prior when I found myself sitting on a public toilet with a little instrument between my legs that looked like a paint brush. I carefully relieved myself upon it while I pleaded with someone – anyone – that this should not be happening to me. When the two negative blue lines appeared I was awash with torrential relief. All I could do then was look at my miserable present and the mess I'd trailed behind that was my past. Yet, when I looked at you on that airplane – even though you could not see me – I saw something I hadn't envisioned before. Call it what you will – happiness, love, bravery – but I saw a future.

No Room at the Inn

Jon Haber

Yes, we'd had a fantastic adventure since the birth of our son, Rafa – on a grey August morning in Edinburgh. We'd dealt with the usual strains of my business in its unhealthy hectic end of season period, we had vital mother in-law help for a month and an overwhelming amount of goodwill from friends and family the world over. Rafa's first three months were a blur of midnight milk feeds, absent father on work trips and the sound of ironic cheers emanating from Tynecastle stadium at the wrong end of Hearts' relegation/insolvency season. He is a true Edinburgh lad!

So in November, we said farewell to our mates during a boozy Yorkshire Three Peaks Challenge, Rafa's contribution was much sleeping in a shabby hostel whilst his dad was playing the piano dressed in a wolf costume.

A few sunny days later, we left Scotland, drove down to London via Staffordshire in our sorry- for-itself Volvo, sold the car for less than a cheap secondhand pushbike (the buyer was robbed, your Honour) and flew out of Heathrow on a bright frosty morning.

Rafa got to spend the next four months meeting all his worldwide Aussie rellies, or most of, or even some of them; exploring the warm damp climate of Ho Chi Min city, the surprisingly temperate Melbourne and the oppressive heat and bush fire risk of rural Victoria. He got to experience his parents' second wedding and got his own Indigenous Australian Welcome to Country. He got to 'swim' in the Boggy Creek and Lake Tyres and the beautiful clear blue waters of Betka Beach. He got to see roos and wallabies, possums, kookaburras and galahs, wombats, bilbies, an emu and a dangerous black snake. The saltwater crocs and great white sharks can wait for a future visit.

He got to dip his toes in the warm end of summer waters of the Pacific Ocean in New Zealand, howl like an orc during a visit to Hobbiton, get a cuddle from a long missed friend at Lake Taupo and another one from his great uncle a few days later on the beach at Santa Cruz, California. He charmed cabin crew and fellow passengers on flights from London to Singapore, HCMC, Melbourne, Auckland, San Fran and back to London. He charmed customers and staff of cafes and diners in Mt Hotham, Eurora, Sale, Inverloch, Mirboo North and many more small Aussie towns; he pulled the same trick in Taupo and Rotorua in NZ and in Rogue River, Florence and Brandon in Oregon. In Banff in Canada, he discovered the social inclusion of the high chair. At Lake Tyers Beach, he discovered irresistible pizza crust and at Nowa Nowa, watermelon.

He spent a glorious hot evening passed out on the floor in front of the TV with his Uncle, mid house renovation and moving project in 40c heat. A few weeks later, he spent the evening evacuated to the beach whilst his family watched news of encroaching bush fires.

He got to experience a real rural Australian cricket club Christmas party where he avoided the initiation of being shoved in a wheelie bin and the genteel Nowa Nowa community party where a somewhat familiar Santa Claus delivered him a present in German, Swedish and Norwegian and where the Grandma-produced cakes were exceptional. He was guest of honour at the city family Christmas party and the country family New Year fest. He attended his first music festival at Mingling Waters and his second one at Fruiteville a few days before leaving Australia.

He got chucked out of every pub and bar he went to in Canada but seemed to be welcomed elsewhere.

He got taken on a short but steep hill walk on the Californian coast in warm early summer sunshine and on a shorter park walk in super cold Calgary a week later. He got time for a cuddle from dad's cousin in San Jose and to eat some sand at Half Moon Bay before the adventures reached their natural end and it was time for us to return to our real lives in Scotland.

It was with quite a bit of uncertainty that we found ourselves crossing the border at Gretna, all be it in a slightly better secondhand car than the battered Volvo of the previous November.

Where were we going to live? What are we doing about office space for the company? Who is doing Ben Nevis at Easter? Where are we staying tonight? Luckily the final question had been fixed by a quick online reservation on the hostelworld website. Rafa was a veteran already of 14 bed nights in the cheaper varieties of American motels and of hostels in NZ, Banff and San Fran so a double private in the Grassmarket backpackers would be 'Nae Bother, Pal' as Rafa is bound to say one day.

As we drove north on the picturesque Moffat Road, the heavens opened. We had a good laugh commenting on Scotland's weather giving him a right royal welcome on his return to the land of his birth whilst the windscreen wipers struggled to cope. It made me wonder, with the referendum coming up, what sort of Scotland would Rafa really be growing up in. With an English dad and an Australian mum, would he be treated as one of the blue shirted team or as a pariah? Will he grow up to be a passionate advocate of Scottish outdoor life like his dad, a born talent for playing rugby like his granddad and uncle or the same talent for Aussie Rules as his maternal granddad and uncle. Will he develop an irrepressible urge to cross uninhabited, snowy Norwegian plateaux like his dad or to swim around sun soaked islands like his mum. Only time will tell.

When we reached Edinburgh, the downpour had ceased, replaced by an evening of cold clear blue sky and weak setting sun. We parked our car in the Grassmarket, surrounded by hordes of stag and hen parties and a few startled lost normal tourists. Of course, with my long history of bargain car purchases, we knew a few things on the recently purchased motor from a Lithuanian dealer in deepest Essex might not be completely functional. As we had found out a few days before, the car has an inoperative locking system so you can't keep valuables hidden or otherwise in the car.

I carried as many of our numerous bags, family heirlooms and baby supplies as possible whilst Sandy took Rafa in the pram to the hostel reception. True to form, Rafa charmed the pleasant receptionists and we were duly installed in our own private room, all be it on floor Nine and Three-Quarters. I remember thinking I hope they never have a fire in this place as we took the lift up, then went up one set of stairs and across a landing before descending to another annex where we found our room. Rafa had a good crawl around his new surroundings, which despite being in a medieval building could still have been in California, Oregon or Canada. I went on a couple of more expeditions to retrieve all the stuff from the car, cursing my naïveté in checking all the usual things like oil, water and tyres and not noticing that Mr. Lithuanian Essex car dealer already had the car open.

Half an hour later we had a sleepy Rafa ready for bed and an apologetic knock on the hostel room door.

'I'm really sorry but it's a strict hostel policy not to allow under sixteens,' announced the pleasant receptionist, slightly embarrassed. I was trying hard not to blow up, citing the lack of age restriction info on the hostelworld site, but thankfully, the receptionist said we could take our time to rebook somewhere else, and we would get a full refund.

So we gave up on hip Scottish hostels *und danach eine Woche ein Zimmer im Motel-One bestillt haben*. At least German efficiency gave us a week to find a flat from a room with curious turquoise blue walls, a functioning lift and a great European breakfast during which Rafa could smile at the other guests and I could read the Scotsman and get Sandy refills of coffee. We even found a nice flat to live in, close to the park and Rafa's favourite swings and still in earshot of Tynecastle during the promotion/new administration season. He is a true Edinburgh lad!

The Prickly Upside

Lydia Teychenne

Thailand

Waiting.

Surveying my surroundings, I find comfort in the room's white walls and grey vinyl floor proving spotless under the harshness of fluorescent light. Inward I am restless, yet I try not to move. A grunt from the plastic bed sheet beneath me is a reminder of the foreignness of my situation. I deliberately shift my thoughts to my breath, focusing on evenness to calm my quickening heart. I smile brightly, wide mouth, showing teeth. The latest inflight magazine proclaims smiling relaxes you.

I feel like an idiot.

Two male nurses enter the room, busying themselves with preparation. A lamp is wheeled over and a stainless steel bin placed at the foot of my bed. I stare at the bin. It has a grate where a lid should be. I consider why.

My doctor enters, pleasant-looking with brown hair and brown eyes. I smile in recognition, cheered to see a familiar face, yet any attempt at social nicety feels absurd. A nurse appears before me, eyes floating over a white mask. He silently guides me to lie down. The plastic bed sheet grumbles. Head resting on a plastic pillow, I am aware I can no longer see my feet. This panics me somewhat. I stare up at the white ceiling.

Seven months ago I gave birth to my baby, I can endure this.

A male nurse holds my leg firmly. I am no longer in control of my situation. The first of three needles is inserted into the soft padding of my right foot in what feels to be a slow and deliberate assault. The shaft is internally moved about as if searching for something.

I cry out, a sound I don't recognise.

Wordlessly, the masked nurse offers a small, brown towel. I take it but am unsure of its purpose. It becomes clear as the doctor inserts a scalpel to begin the bloody task of removing the shards of sea urchin imbedded in my sole. With a clenched fist I shove the towel into my face. Feeling a mixture of embarrassment and panic, I use the brown towel to hide from the scrutiny of the fluorescent above.

I have a moment of relief. Cool water tingles my foot.

I comprehend the need for the grate on which my foot rests. I attempt to say something jovial to the room, an apology for being such a sook. My Australian colloquialism is lost. I feel alone and my thoughts drift to my friends, waiting for me on the other side of the wall. I fear that my son and I have become an encumbrance to the trip. In joining my friends on this overseas adventure, I'd hoped to prove to myself that life with a baby could still have remnants of yesterday. I had felt brave in my decision to come.

A second needle is inserted into the centre of my foot, continuing the unsympathetic search.

I cry out. Louder this time.

I worry that my son can hear me.

Where is my coping mechanism for enduring pain?

Lapsed yoga membership and a preference for morning coffee over meditation contribute to an inability to control my cries. I recall being unable to find my coping mechanism during labour either, a rather startling realisation after imagining one would naturally discover strength not yet tested. The difference was that during labour, naked and watching the clock, I felt easy in my lone adventure.

In the sterile white room, I feel alone.

Underneath the brown towel, my eyes are squeezed shut, trying not to visualize each cut, flick and scrape. The doctor senses my struggle and clears his throat. The cooling effect of water has vanished. The scalpel's marks feel raw and open. I am worn-out.

The doctor looks at his watch, mindful of the curfew, reminding me of the recent military coup. He quickly inserts a third needle into the ball of my foot. A sense of hopelessness washes over me. The towel absorbs salty tears. The doctor works more quickly now, sensing my disappearing resolve.

I failed.

I was unable to keep myself safe, and now my friends have to look after my baby and me. *On their holiday.* The thought of our imposition makes me shrink in shame. My independence and bravery were short-lived. I now need to ask others to carry my baby, to bath him and swim with him.

The doctor begins to bandage my foot. I'm told I need to keep the wounds dry for a week. *I'm in Thailand in 35 degree weather and I am not allowed to swim.* The thought of wearing a nappy bag to protect my foot is appalling.

Through the walls I can hear my friends in song, amusing Eden as they wait for my release. I remove the towel. My eyes remain closed as they adjust to the light and inwardly I adjust to the idea of dependence.

Laughter.

I hear Eden's distinct ring. He's enjoying being the centre of attention. Wheeled outside, I am greeted boisterously by my friends as if I were joining an afternoon session at the local pub. I am cheered by the sight of Eden who sits comfortably on the hip of another. On the bus, I watch as another

126

friend wears Eden in a sling, holding him close and whispering songs in his ear until he falls asleep.

Gratitude pushes aside self-pity and shame.

My friends now have an opportunity to care for Eden. Through care, there is the opportunity to love. Eden won't remember this international adventure, his ride on an elephant through the wet jungles in Krabi or the noisy tuk tuk trips through the city of Bangkok. Yet, shared between the hips of four Australians as we explore Thai beaches and towns, Eden's world has opened up.

Eden's world is now bigger than just me.

I Carried You Both

Erin Mckittrick

Alaska

My daughter, I asked about you. Should I bring you? 300 miles of Arctic shoreline. Sand and bears and bugs and wind storms, and I might walk ten miles in a day, from the wild to the wilder.

'Why not?' the midwives said.

'Listen to your body,' they said.

I listened. To the screaming murres, and the synthetic roar of my nylon raincoat flapping in the wind. To the crackling fire and the lapping waves of the Chukchi Sea. And when it was quiet, I tried to listen to you. You were just a swish and a wiggle inside me – the rounding that stopped me from buckling a waistbelt, and sent my stomach muscles into spasms when I paddled too hard. You whipped my metabolism into a furnace, driving off the chill when the rain blew in off the Arctic Ocean, and dripped into the crevices of my clothes. You were quiet. You were as warm and safe as I was.

My son, you were a different matter. You were a shriek in my ear that could out-scream the kittiwakes, sippy cup dribbles in my hair, and compostable diapers incinerated on a wind-whipped fire. You rode on my back, using my shoulder as a pillow. You played in the sand, using my shoes as your toys. You were loud, messy, heavy and still so very small.

You toddled along in the tracks of grizzly bears, and I could see that their feet were as big as your head.

I didn't know anyone to ask before I brought you. No professional I could turn to, and say 'Can I carry my baby for a month through the cold, wet, bear-infested wilderness? Is it crazy? Is it safe?' And we brought all the raingear and snacks and snuggles, and set off to ask the only people we could.

We asked the Alaska Natives in the villages we passed through. They fed you whale blubber, and said that 'My grandparents travelled like that.' Or: 'When I was a boy, my family herded reindeer all across that country.' They passed us strips of dried caribou, frozen fish, and boiled beluga, and shared their stories. Beyond the villages, we asked the crumbling middens and graveyards marked with whale bones, and I imagined what those ancestors could have told us. Families have always lived here. Mothers have always walked with their babies on their backs.

You strung together your first sentences that summer, about leaning trees and paddling in rivers and bears that eat fish. But you never list that journey when you tell of all the trips you've done. You've forgotten. I hold those memories for you.

We're on an airplane right now, with parkas and skis and mittens all packed for an adventure you're both old enough to anticipate, with eager chatter and little fingers tracing along the edge of an Alaska map.

And maybe you'd be old enough, this time, to tell the stories yourselves.

But the swaying rhythm of all those steps I carried you is still there – etched into each of your souls. Those forgotten rhythms build a person, like the sing-song of all those story books and nursery rhymes you were also too young to remember.

> *You'll know golden-pink tundra and muddy bear tracks.*
> *Crackling fires and bags full of snacks.*
> *The screams of the gulls, and the wild berries tang.*
> *Bad notes in the hundreds of rhymes that I sang.*
> *The sting of the wind and the taste of the sand.*
> *The exuberant rush of the wide open land.*
>
> *You won't remember, but you'll understand.*

Biographies

Anne Hamilton

Anne Hamilton is a creative writing tutor and fiction editor who lives in Edinburgh with her young son. She has a PhD in Creative Writing from the University of Glasgow, and is the editor of online magazine, *Lothian Life*, and the author of travel memoir, *A Blonde Bengali Wife*, which inspired the Bangladesh-based charity, Bhola's Children. Anne's short stories are published online and in several anthologies; she was the winner of the New Asian Writing short story competition 2016 and has been shortlisted for a Fresher Writing Award 2016. Anne has just completed her first novel.

Find Anne at: www.writerightediting.co.uk

http://anne-ablondebengaliwife.blogspot.co.uk/

Rick Rutjens

Rick Rutjens has been a writer for as long as he can remember. He grew up in a hamlet of four houses. There were no other kids his age.

He wrote to invent the adventures he'd be having if a) there had been other kids and b) he hadn't been dysfunctionally shy.

He now writes words for other people and gets paid for it. He lives on a hill overlooking the hamlet. He has no neighbours.

Sylvain Morisot

Wait, should we start by who am I or who I think I am, hmm tough question and easy answer. I believe I am a seasoned traveller with plenty of luck to do a job that can let me go wherever I want. Destination varies but must always involve playing baseball at some point. How did a boy from the French countryside end up playing baseball, well let's say one movie made me, Bull Durham. So from countryside to bigger cities to Japan then to Scotland then to Australia I made many friends playing baseball and I am keeping the dice rolling with two good additions, my girlfriend Nadia and our little monster Isabella.

Sarah Dyer

Born in South Wales in the mid 1960's, Dyer left home at the age of 17 to work in London.

She has always written fiction but until studying for her Masters in Creative Writing (which lead to her liberation from her 14 year marriage) she was terribly shy about sharing it.

Exploring emotional truth and the concept of belonging (Hiraeth in Welsh) within her fiction, her prose and poetry celebrate the feminine.

Dyer has lived in Vietnam, Thailand, Singapore, Indonesia, Malaysia and Aberdeen, though is settled now in Edinburgh with her two sons and rescue dog.

Meghan J. Ward

Based in Banff, Canada, Meghan J. Ward is a freelance writer and the co-founder/Editor-in-Chief at Crowfoot Media, a mountain culture publishing house. Living in the heart of the Canadian Rockies gives her access to some of the world's most beautiful landscapes and offers her year-round inspiration. An avid adventurer, her pre-parenthood travels took her backpacking in the Caribbean, ski touring in the Arctic, climbing throughout the Canadian Rockies and trekking in Nepal. Now, she and her husband Paul Zizka are dedicated to travelling abroad each year with their daughter, Mistaya, and have so far visited New Zealand, Niue, French Polynesia, Hawaii and Belize. Follow her projects and journey at meghanjoy-ward.com.

Stuart A. Paterson

Stuart A. Paterson, born 1966, is a widely published & anthologised Scottish poet. A past recipient of an Eric Gregory Award & a Robert Louis Stevenson Fellowship, his 2015 collection of poems about Dumfries & Galloway, 'Border Lines' (Indigo Dreams), was voted Best Poetry Pamphlet at the 2016 Saboteur Awards in London. His latest collection is 'Aye', poems in Scots, published by Tapsalteerie. He lives by the Galloway coast.

More info available at: facebook.com/patersonpoetry/

Sophie Isaacson

Aged 24 and mum of 4 month old baby Teddy; Sophie Isaacson is a part-time Youth Development Coordinator with a passion for writing, adventuring and photography. Sophie has grown up on the remote island of Tiree off the West coast of Scotland and is currently working her way through an English Degree with the Open university. Sophie loves being outside with her baby boy and dog, enjoys travelling, taking photos, making jewellery and learning new things.

Find Sophie at: www.sofiescribbles.com

Nicky Torode

Nicky Torode is a teacher, trainer in personal development, coach and writer. She has written academic articles for journals, including the International Journal on Minority Rights and various human rights NGO publications. She recently wrote Sorted – Coaching for Teenagers and several book reviews published in leadership and coaching magazines.

She is currently enjoying writing more creative pieces including flash fiction stories and travel writing.

Sarah C. Thewlis

Sarah is an Edinburgh-based writer and recent English Literature graduate from Oxford University. She grew up in Alicante, Spain, where she had her first experience of professional writing at the age of 14, after her novel, *A Taste of Sky*, was commissioned by Libros International. She is currently working on her next novel, *Margery and Pain*, as well as the libretto for *Markheim*, a new musical based on the work of R. L. Stevenson, written in collaboration with a composer at the Royal College of Music.

Find Sarah at: sarahcthewlis.com

Cecile Sophie Bec
Cecile is from Lincolnshire, and studies Jewellery and Metal Design and Duncan of Jordanstone College of Art and Design in Dundee. Before moving to Dundee, she was living in Edinburgh where she worked in the Filmhouse Bar.

Cecile has been inspired to write for a while and is glad to have taken the plunge by writing a short story. She now writes a blog called 'Cecile' loosely based on her experiences as a student in Dundee.

Read it at: cecilesophie17.wordpress.com

Sandy Bennett-Haber
An Edinburgh based Australian writer. Sandy received Bachelor of Arts (Hons) Creative Writing from Monash University. Sandy became a backpacker at thirty. She blogged her way around the world in 2011 before coming to rest in Scotland. She now has a husband and two young sons to travel with. Sandy has had a small handfull of fiction published in collections in Australia and Scotland and still manages an occasional blog on flamingorover.blogspot. co.uk

Marcia Ulrich
Marcia is a well travelled and adventurous spirit from Michigan, USA. She is a mother and a doting Grandmother who seeks out fun and friendship in the world around her.

Gary Yelen

(sculptor, painter, builder of stuff and occasional writer).
Gary has lived in East Gippsland since 1995, along the way to the present day he established Yelens Studio Gallery, along the shores of Lake Tyers, initiated, curated, contributed and partnered in many and varied arts projects. Before this he lived overseas, in Israel where he honed his sculptural skills, established a partnership in the Brushwood Studios in the Republic of Ireland and exhibited, worked and sold in Europe, U.S.A, Middle East and Australia.

He now lives part time in France establishing Frukt studios and workshop, exhibiting works and developing an arts residency program.

As well as contributing a story for this collection Gary's painting 'You and Your Boy' has been used for the cover art.

See Gary's artwork and French adventuring at: frukt. com.au

David Wilkie

As a poet, David's journey began over two decades ago, when he was inspired to write a few humorous words after the death of a former work colleague. From that day to the present, David finds inspiration in all manner of subjects, however it is life and love that he finds most inspiring. To date Wilke has had work published within 47 anthologies. Poetic highlights include being guest poet speaker at the Aberdeen Wallace Event in 2005 before HRH. In 2006 Wilkie published 'In my own write: Scotland, a land o' Warrior Poets.'

Jo Smith

Jo Smith lives near Biggar in Scotland and enjoys writing poems and short stories about family life and the ups and downs of contemporary daily experience. The undertones and subtleties of relationships which are often overlooked in the hurry of modern living fire her imagination to capture those stories which lie just beneath the surface of our public lives. The arrival of a baby brings many challenges both practical and emotional, especially for a young mother, making the bond between parent and baby journeying together 'against the world' especially strong.

Helen Sheil

Helen's writing encompasses seemingly diverse genres of academic writing on rural policy, regional development and transformative community engagement to personal poems. In both she strives to convey (albeit to different audiences) the connections between people and the landscapes they inhabit. Rural lifestyle is often on the fringe of planning while also the source of renewal –something we love but leave to others to look after. Her poems share snapshots of these people and places while her academic writing unpacks practice which can integrate urban and rural areas as partners in dynamic regions. She is currently developing a style which takes the personal into the academic – a skill some have well-honed in an authentic mother tongue.

Stacey Campbell

Stacey Campbell graduated with a degree in History from the University of Glasgow in 2015. Always a keen writer, her storytelling was sparked by a childhood love of Roald Dahl and the power of her imagination to conjure impossible things. Still a lover of Roald Dahl and all things strange, she lives her life by the motto 'be kind, thankful and bold'. In her free time, she enjoys reading Sylvia Plath, walking her dog and planning her next adventure. She is an ardent feminist and writes on a variety of topics.

Read more at www.stardustresidue.com.

Jon Haber

Translator, IT worker and Mountain Leader; Jonathan Haber never expected to become a married father in his mid 40s – the all-consuming stress of running a small adventure travel business for 15 years had put paid to that. However, he always had and always will find inspiration in the adventure and travel parts.

He harbours a not so secret desire to return to Norway at some point and involve Sandy, Rafa and Finn in cross country skiing and snow camping escapades. His Scottish adventures are at www.walkaboutscotland.com

Lydia Teychenne

Lydia is a creative producer within Australia's performing arts industry. She has worked throughout Australia and internationally across a range of interdisciplinary arts projects including large-scale interactive public art projects, digital arts, gallery commissions, contemporary dance, music and theatre projects. Lydia has developed tri-continental projects and complex international collaborations between Australia, Europe and Asia. Before becoming a mum, Lydia worked with many major arts festivals and organisations and toured extensively on the international festival circuit. Since becoming a mum, Lydia consults with independent artists and the OzAsia Festival while completing her Masters in Diplomacy and Trade, in pursuit of strengthening Cultural diplomacy for Australian artists working internationally. Her contribution to this collection is Lydia's first work of creative non-fiction.

Erin McKittrick

Erin McKittrick is a writer, adventurer and scientist based in Seldovia, Alaska, and author of "A Long Trek Home: 4,000 Miles by Boot, Raft and Ski" and "Small Feet, Big Land: Adventure, Home and Family on the Edge of Alaska." You can find her at GroundTruthTrekking.org.

The Thank You Page

Many of the ideas and plans a person with a baby has flounder under the tidal pull of day to day struggle to get by. This book could very easily have been just one more bit of lost flotsam were it not for the combined efforts of all the writers who contributed work. My thanks to each and every one of you for entrusting me with your stories.

A special warm thanks goes to the Edinburgh contributors who hung out with the children and I and chatted writing, babies and travel. And to all my Australian friends and family for always keeping us in your hearts.

Thanks to Bronwyn Tutty for being you, Sarah C. Thewlis for book chats, Edinburgh Creative Writing Co-Op for being my writing home when I first arrived in Edinburgh, Creative Scotland for helping me link in to so many talented writers.

All libraries everywhere, (borrow a book) but especially our local – Fountainbridge Library.

Thanks to Sheila Wakefield of Red Squirrel Press and Jeremy Webb of Webb Active Media for generosity to the project.

Thanks to Anne Hamilton's Write*Right* editing services and her general willingness to talk about the book's (sometimes non-existent) progress, and her willingness to stand around in the snow while our boys jump on the trampoline. Go to www.writerightediting.co.uk if you are a writer who needs a constructive and kind ear.

Thanks to my soul sisters Lydia and Helen – for sharing the adventures of youth and university and motherhood with me. Somehow our travels have landed us at different points across the globe and we had to meet each others sons for the first time over Skype – but nevertheless I look forward to the next beer we share together and revisiting our Willsons Promontory lighthouse hike.

Thanks to my mum and dad for encouraging adventuring from a young age.

Thanks to my husband for going on this journey with me, and to our sons Rafa and Finn for journeying with us.